BORGLUND, Erland, 1894-

Working in plastic, bone, amber, and horn. [By] Erland Borglund & Jacob Flauensgaard. [Ed. in English by Clara Fried Zwiebel] N.Y., Reinhold [c1968]
96p. illus. (Reinhold Scandinavian craft series)

(See next card)

WORKING IN PLASTIC, BONE, AMBER, AND HORN

ERLAND BORGLUND AND
JACOB FLAUENSGAARD

REINHOLD BOOK CORPORATION
A subsidiary of Chapman-Reinhold, Inc.
NEW YORK AMSTERDAM LONDON

Printed in the United States of America
Library of Congress Catalog Card Number 67–24691

Typeset, printed, and bound by The Guinn Company, Inc.
Edited in English by Clara Fried Zwiebel
Published by Reinhold Book Corporation
A subsidiary of Chapman-Reinhold, Inc.
430 Park Avenue, New York, N. Y. 10022

Contents

Plastic, Bone, Amber, and Horn

Artifacts of bone, amber, and horn were fashioned far back in the history of mankind. Natural History museums abound with jewelry and tools made by our forefathers who early discovered the potential strength and beauty in these natural materials. Contemporary handicraft exhibits contain innumerable examples of present-day work in the very same materials that were used by the Stone Age man. Jewelry of bone, amber, and horn made by modern craftsmen is available everywhere in local shops. These are materials which may change in style but will, like jewel stones, always remain with us in pure form. The methods of working them have been handed down through the ages from primitive artisans to urban craftsmen who have shaped these materials into fine objects of daily use. The transition today to the hobbyist's workshop is really quite natural for this interesting craft; traditions extending back through the centuries have caught up with our leisure-time culture. That commercial upstart, plastic, has been included with bone, amber, and horn in this book because it is worked in much the same way. It must be admitted that industry with its unlimited mass production of plastic products may intimidate us a little into thinking of plastic as a rather soulless material for artwork. There have been so many poor plastic things made, both garish and badly designed, nevertheless, used properly, plastic has a great many possibilities, particularly for beautifully formed practical objects. These should be judged not only from an aesthetic viewpoint but from a functional standpoint as well.

In the section on plastics in this book, there are many suggestions for making attractive household utensils which are certainly conversation pieces for the proud hobbyist who personally made them! The more aesthetic of the projects have been turned over to the raw materials of greater value such as horn and amber but might just as well be done in plastic. The real potential of these four materials assures them becoming increasingly popular as craft media.

Examples of antique pieces made of horn.

Plastic

What is plastic? Where does it come from? What can it be used for?

These questions have been considered time after time in the last fifty years and have incited inventive people to develop new plastics to a high degree thereby taking their rightful place as a fine, yet inexpensive, contemporary craft material.

The possibilities seem to be unlimited. Every day something new which has been molded, poured, or pressed from plastic is introduced on the market.

The first usable plastic was made nearly a hundred years ago—a fact that probably may come as a surprise to many.

In his experiments to find a substitute for ivory which was very expensive and in short supply, an American inventor, John Hyatt, in 1872, discovered a compound which he called celluloid. His initial intention was to discover a substance for making cheaper billiard balls but the new material was found to have a far greater potential. Toilet articles, book bindings, dolls and games, the famous washable men's stiff shirt collars, etc., were now made from celluloid. But this new discovery was found to be dangerously inflammable. Scientists went on with their research to find a similar, yet safer, material. In the early 1900s in Germany, Adolph Spitteler developed a type of plastic using junket powder as the primary ingredient. A short time later another German, Otto Röhm, was successful in making a transparent type of plastic, but twenty years passed before this plastic was produced cheaply enough for the general market.

In the meantime Dr. Baekeland, a Belgian scientist, created a practical plastic. He emigrated from Belgium to America where he finally succeeded in his plastic research. The material he compounded was called Bakelite and it was used for automobile parts, handles, cases for instruments, radios, boxes, picnic plates, etc. Plastic had now achieved a good foothold, and gradually with continued research, new types began to appear with entirely new characteristics.

The Second World War sped up the process. The rising shortages in wood and metal, with priorities going to war production, created an acute need for new substitute materials. With the various new types of plastic, industry was quickly able to relieve the situation.

One important type of plastic is *acrylic* plastic known by the trade names of Plexiglas or Lucite.

In contrast to the thermosetting plastic (a hardened state which will not remelt), acrylic plastic is pliable when reheated, which means it is a thermoplastic. It is clear as glass, less breakable, easy to work with, and has many other unusual properties such as the quality of bending light which will enter at one end of a *solid* plastic tube and come out at the other. It is surprising to see what splendid objects you can make with it using very simple tools.

On the following pages there are directions for working with the material. Because we have found that plastic is becoming more and more popular as a hobby material, many objects that are both useful around the home and also fun and stimulating to work with are described. Plastic is simple to handle and both children and adults are finding great pleasure in working with it. There is now a new type of plastic specially created for hobby use called *Polyester Casting Resin.* In recent years this plastic has been used for a great number of projects. The method of using this polyester resin is discussed in a special section beginning on page 45.

Material

The acrylic plastic (Lucite or Plexiglas) which is used for these projects is available in sheets of various thicknesses, in round bars and hollow tubes as well as in cord and in a flat band-shape excellent for basketry. It can be obtained in clear plastic or dyed in transparent, opaque, or fluorescent colors. Clear polyester casting resin is also widely available. Any of these can be purchased in a well-stocked hobby shop or from special artcraft suppliers listed on page 96.

Tools

The necessary tools to work the plastic can usually be found in the average tool box. It should be pointed out, however, that good tools, if it is necessary to buy those you do not have, will pay for themselves in the long run and your finished pieces will reflect the quality of the tools used.

Large power tools, of course, will always make part of the work easier, but only rarely will they make the results more beautiful.

Tools for Working with Plastic:

Vise.

Coping saw and V-support.

Saws: Handsaw; hacksaw or backsaw; coping saw or jeweler's saw with metalworking saw blades Nos. 0 to 5.

Hand drill or brace-and-bit with twist drills for metal, sizes 1/32″, 1/16″, 1/8″, bradawl or scriber.

Crosscut hand files (fine and coarse) with various profiles.

File card or file cleaner.
Small flat-nose and round-nose pliers.
Sandpaper: Nos. 1, 1/0, 2/0 (coarse, medium, fine).

Preparation

Acrylic plastic is worked in the same way as is bone or wood. The first tools used are the handsaw and wood file. The grinding and polishing is done with sandpaper. Buffing methods are described on page 14. Without too great an effort and a little patience, you can obtain good results.

This material is as transparent as glass, but it will not break easily and you will not cut yourself with it as you might with glass.

Plastic is easy to work and demands no final surface finish after polishing. It does not absorb moisture.

Acrylic plastic's special characteristics make it particularly useful for many things since it is easily rendered pliable with the application of heat, it is hard-wearing, and has an unusual resistance to blows.

Always protect the shiny surface of the plastic! This material has high luminosity, thus nicks and scratches on the surface will show up clearly. Before acrylic plastic sheets are sent out of the factory, they are given a protective paper coating on both sides. This is adhered with rubber cement or gelatin and it ought to be left on as long as possible while you are working with it. If it comes off, it should be cemented on again before proceeding to the next step. Try to use rubber cement, not a glue that may dissolve the plastic surface and make the paper adhere permanently. If you are going to heat the plastic, however, remove all the paper and every bit of rubber cement for the smallest particle of cement or glue can create ugly brown spots when heated.

Cutting

In working with the thinnest sheets of acrylic plastic (1/8″ or less) you can use practically the same cutting technique as is used for ordinary glass. With a bodkin, bradawl, scriber, or engraver's marker, deeply incise the cutting line. Leave the protective paper in place and use a steel ruler to guide your hand, holding it securely against the plastic (see photograph, p. 10). Lay the piece of incised plastic along the edge of the worktable. With a protective piece of wood on top, clamp it to the table edge along the marked line, then, with a strong pair of pliers, break the plastic downward along the line.

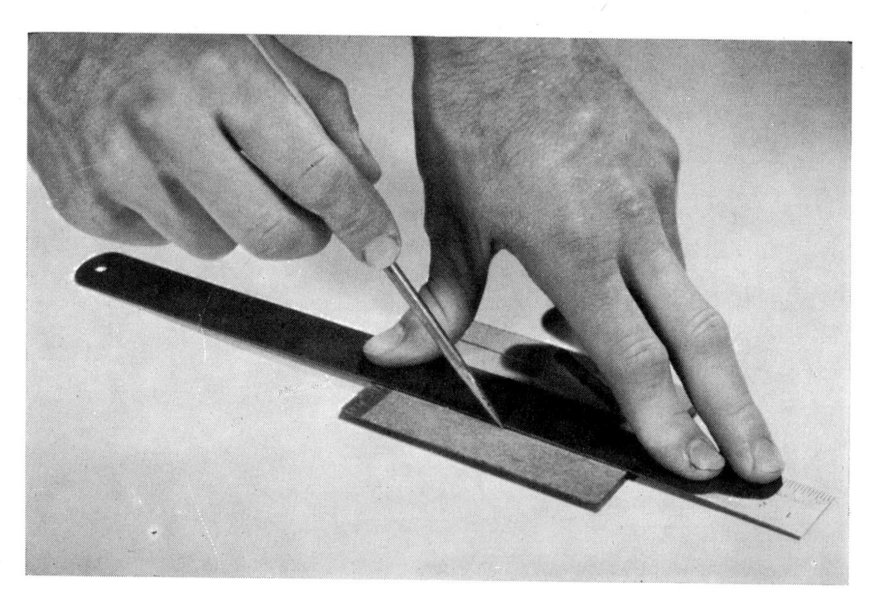

Incising.

This method is only practical for smaller pieces which are not more than 8″ or 10″ long. For longer pieces it is better to use a saw.

Sawing

Use only sharp tools. If you use a dull or blunted saw blade the friction will heat the plastic and the saw teeth will cake up. When using a power saw pause frequently and work slowly to minimize friction heating.

Hand Sawing

Choose a saw that is best suited to the work. If the saw is too coarse it will spoil the edge. Before beginning to saw, draw a line on the protective paper coating as a guide for the saw. If there is no paper you can make a line with the scriber or bradawl directly on the surface of the plastic.

Sawing Straight Lines

In sawing straight lines use the hacksaw or a backsaw. Hold the plastic securely. Make sure that it does not move while you are sawing. Avoid too hard a pressure on the saw (see photograph, p. 11).

Sawing Curved Lines

Use a coping saw or jeweler's saw. Work on a coping saw V-block (see photograph, p. 13).

Sawing Bars or Tubes

Fasten these in a vise, but take the precaution of putting a piece of heavy cardboard between the jaws of the vise and the plastic so it will not mar. Avoid screwing the vise too tightly. Use a hacksaw for cutting, or a backsaw.

Sawing with Power Tools

Use a fine-toothed band or circular saw for power sawing of plastic.
Band saw:
Width of blade: ⅜″-¾″.
Thickness: 1/32″-1/16″.
Teeth: ⅛″ with minimum set.

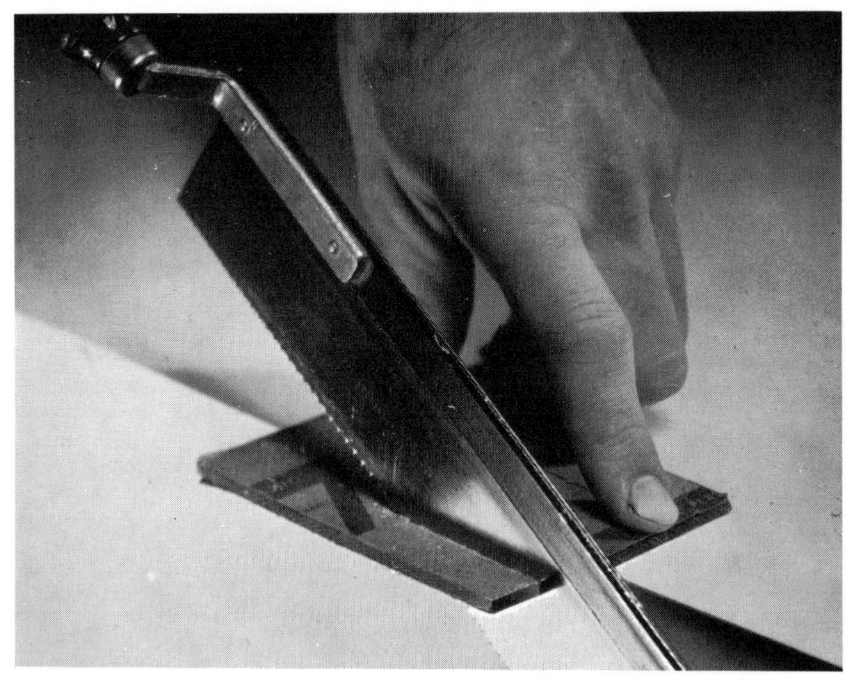

Sawing with the backsaw.

File the sawed edge gently with a hand file or buffer to avoid nicking the edges. Remember to allow for this necessary step when measuring your piece.

Surface Treatment of Acrylic Plastic

After sawing, the edges will be rough and dull and they must be finished in a special way. Begin as you would start to work on wood, using a plane, wood file, and sandpaper.

Planing

It is best to plane only the thicker acrylic plastic. Begin by protecting the plastic in the vise with a layer of cardboard, as suggested earlier. Make sure your cutter blade is sharp and very finely adjusted. Plane quite carefully. If shavings stick to the cutter blade, they must be removed with a cloth dipped in thinner.

Filing

Using an ordinary wood file, stroke away from your body. You can file a small piece of plastic holding it in your hand, but larger pieces should be fastened in a vise. Always protect the sides of the plastic being worked with heavy paper or cardboard.

After the first rough filing, you can switch to a metal file with finer teeth. For very small or intricate pieces, use a jeweler's or a needle file.

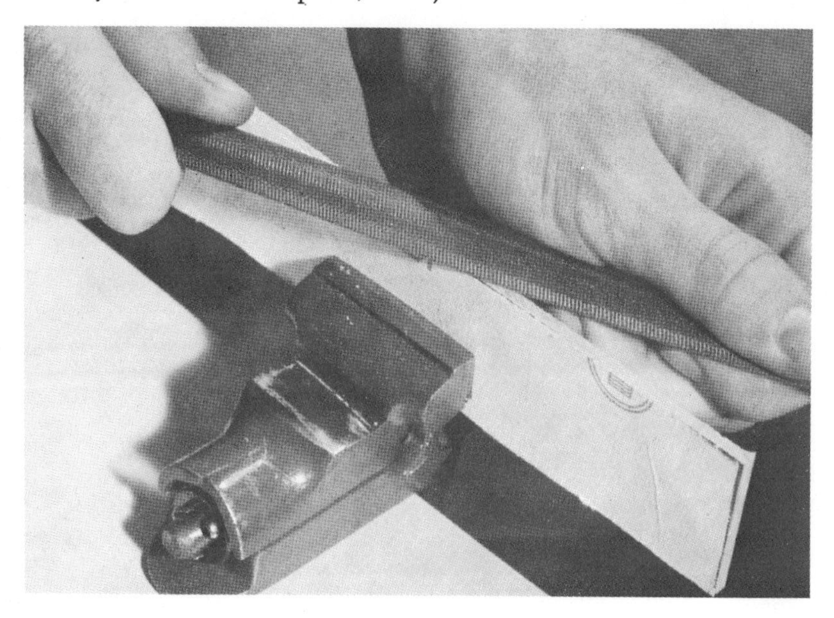

Sawing plastic.

Whether you use a coping saw or a hacksaw, you must work carefully so that the plastic does not clog the teeth of the saw blade.

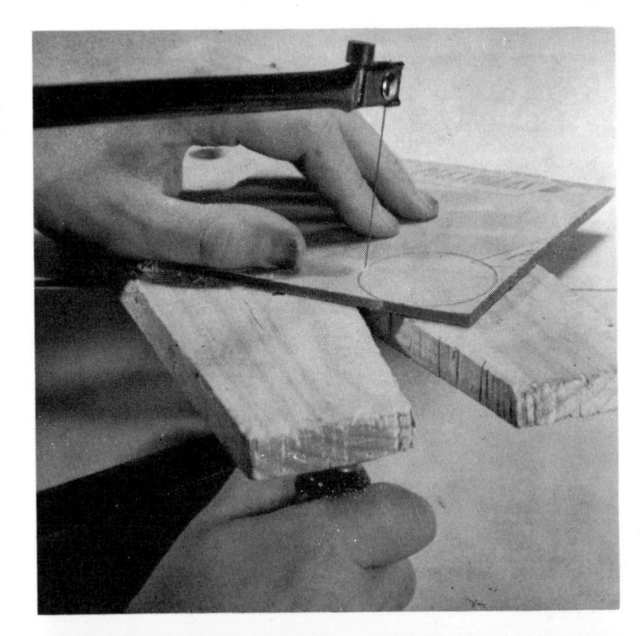

Planing plastic.

The cutting blade of the plane must be very sharp and as finely adjusted as possible.

Opposite page:

Large plastic pieces should be fastened in a vise when being worked. Protect the sides of the plastic with cardboard or heavy paper.

Sanding

Rub the plastic with sandpaper of various grain. Begin with the coarse No. 1 and gradually change to the finer sandpaper, 1/0 and 2/0. The sandpaper should be wrapped around a wood or cork block to give you better control. For the last step use a dampened, very fine-grained, waterproof sandpaper. The result will be a velvety surface that is easily polished.

Scraping

A scraper can be used to remove any file marks if they are not too coarse. The edge should be honed smooth before starting to scrape.

Buffing (Rough Polishing)

Do not begin to polish the plastic until all sanding is completed. If any saw marks appear during the polishing, you will have to sand or scrape a little more until the result is satisfactory. Clean the plastic with a sponge that has been dampened in water containing a few drops of detergent. Then rub the edges with No. 00 steel wool and polish the piece by hand on a mechanized buffing wheel.

Hand Buffing

For polishing use a fine-grained abrasive powder. It can simply be pumice and chalk dissolved in a little water, or a commercial metal polishing cream (it must not, however, contain any ingredients that will dissolve plastic). A polishing powder made especially for plastic, bone, and horn is available on the market.

Apply the powder with a soft cloth then polish with a clean dry cloth until the piece is clear and transparent.

Machine Buffing

If you have access to a buffing wheel it will, of course, speed up the process and give your piece a fast, high shine. Use a soft, stitched-cloth buff together with a suitable buffing compound, available in various brand names. One designed especially for plastic is best.

While buffing the piece hold it lightly in your hand and do not press too hard against the wheel. Move the piece back and forth particularly if the motor runs fast, so the piece will not become overheated and, consequently, be spoiled.

Final Polishing

The shiny surface can be given an even greater luster if it is rubbed with an acrylic plastic polish. For ordinary objects this is probably unnecessary, but in some cases it may be desirable to have a highly glossy surface. To preserve and protect the surface you can use a thin coating of good paste wax.

Static Electricity

Acrylic plastic becomes charged with static electricity when it is rubbed, and this attracts dust particles which stick to the surface. Continued rubbing with a dry cloth makes it even more magnetic. Therefore, you should always use a damp linen cloth or a dampened chamois to clean off the dust. There are anti-static-electricity powders on the market which can be used to help prevent this from occurring on exhibit cases, etc.

Turning

A piece of plastic can be turned on a lathe, but you must make certain that the lathe chisel is firmly fastened or held firmly by hand. Lubricate abundantly with soapy water during the turning. Choose a round plastic rod and place the cutting chisel so that it *scrapes* off the shavings. If you do not have a turning lathe, you can mount the piece on an electric drill rig—if it is a small piece—but do not let it revolve too rapidly.

Threading

This is not a difficult job. Simply use a tap to cut the threads in the holes, but do not use one with too fine a threading. Plastic screws can be made with the same equipment.

Drilling

Ordinarily metal drills are fine for drilling in plastic. Both in hand drilling and in drilling with power tools, you must work much more slowly than when drilling in wood or metal. Do not press too hard. Remove the drill often, clean it of shavings and let it cool. If the drill becomes too warm it will become clogged with melted plastic exactly as in using the saw. Be especially careful at the end of the drilling in order to avoid breakage at the point where the drill emerges from the plastic. It is a better idea to drill inward from both sides.

While drilling, the plastic should be fastened down (see photograph, p. 16), and it is a good idea to place a piece of wood directly under the plastic. The drilled hole will have a dull, frosty appearance inside, but if you want it to be shiny simply add a few drops of turpentine or thin oil into the hole as you work. To make larger holes, it is best to start with a smaller drill, then enlarge this same hole using a larger drill bit.

It is also practical to make the holes after the piece has been polished to avoid having the polishing powder collect in the drilled holes.

To prepare a countersink in the holes, work into them again for a few turns with a larger drill bit—one that corresponds in size to the head of the screw to be used (see drawing).

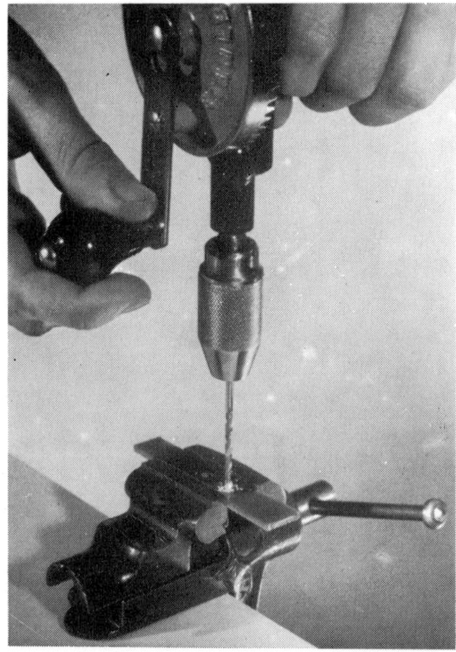

Decorating

Plastic objects may be handsome enough without any further adornment provided they have been designed with a pleasing shape and have been well made. If further decoration is desired, however, one of the following techniques may be used.

Engraving

Tools must be sharp for engraving acrylic plastic. To begin, draw your pattern on a piece of paper. Remove the protective layers of paper from both sides of the plastic and cement your design to the *underside* with rubber cement so that the design is visible through the plastic. Engrave the design on the upper side of the plastic with a sharp instrument—an engraving tool, a bodkin, bradawl, linoleum cutter, or a pen-size electric drill with a long lead, etc. Do not experiment with something you just happen to have in your tool box.

The engraved design made in this manner will be "frosty" and it may either be left alone or filled-in with color.

Framing and Inlaying

Flat pieces only, should be used for this work.

To prepare the frame you can use 3/16″ sheet plastic. The inner edge of the frame piece should have a slight bevel slanting outward toward the underside. A corresponding bevel is filed on the piece to be set in, making its underside slightly larger. The bevels must effect an even contact. The frame and insert can each be of the same or of a different color plastic.

Warm up the frame (15 minutes at 122° F.), then quickly place it on top of the other piece, pressing both together between two smooth pieces of wood. Fasten these, both plastic and protective wood, in a vise.

Let this stand until completely cooled. The soft, warm plastic frame will form a joint with the other piece and hold it in place. If the wood pieces used to press the plastic are smooth enough you will have less polishing work to do later (see drawing, p. 18; *A* and *B* show the bevels).

Note that in making an *inlay,* you need bevel only the insert, the smallest piece, *C*.

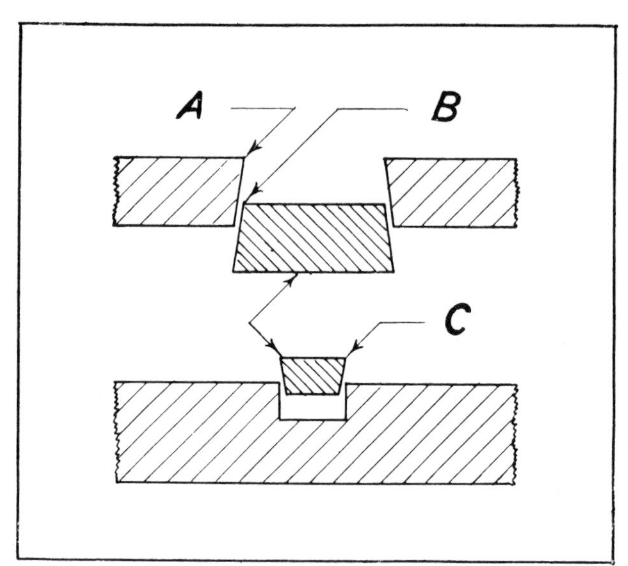

Top sketch shows the framing process. A and B show the bevel. Bottom sketch shows the inlay process. C is the bevel to be made on the inlay piece only. In both cases the piece being set-in is indicated by narrower cross-hatching.

Frosty Surface

You can create a decorative frosty surface on the plastic by sanding it. Experiment with the various grades of sandpaper, but always sand it in the *same* direction.

Carving Designs in Acrylic Plastic

A pen-size, electric or machine drill, which is used pen-fashion, in much the same way as a dentist uses his drill, will simplify this task. A pointed drill, as described earlier in the section on engraving, should be used. The carving is done from the bottom, or reverse of the piece of plastic, and you can create very finely detailed designs such as flowers, birds, fish, or monograms with this technique. Make as few holes as possible with the drill and proceed by working outward from these. Do not let the drill pierce the top surface of the plastic or the whole piece will be ruined. In making these internal carvings in small objects, it is easier to work if the drill is held steady and the *plastic* is moved in the desired direction. The details of the design may later be painted with a fine brush, or they can be left as they are with the frosty engraved effect on the surface.

A thin sheet of clear plastic can be cemented to the bottom to level the piece or to protect the carving. Colored plastic could be effectively used for this. Sand the bottom of the piece with fine sandpaper first so that its surface is absolutely smooth. You may prefer to use colored cement (see below), but then you must select the same color as that of the plastic sheet which you are cementing to the piece.

The final polishing of the cemented sheet should be done after 24 hours of drying time have elapsed.

Painting

Painting on acrylic plastic is done in the same way as painting on wood. Cellulose paints may be used, but do not put on too thick a coat as the acetone in the paint is apt to dissolve the plastic. Since this paint dries fast, the risk is too great. There is, however, the possibility of another problem; the paint may crack if there is a strain on the plastic, if, for example, it has been bent or formed. But if you place the plastic in an oven (122° F) for about a half hour before painting, that risk will be greatly diminished. Oil lacquers can also be used, but the drying time, naturally, is longer for these and there is no real advantage in using it.

Surface Dyeing

These plastics may be dyed with the cold dip dyes that are available at hobby shops. The clean plastic piece is dipped or left in the dye until the desired color is obtained. It is far better, however, to buy uniformly colored plastic, as this surface dyeing is not color-fast to sun and wear.

Dyed Cement

The plastic cement available in hobby shops is colorless. The plastic dyes mentioned above are best suited for dyeing cement and you can obtain excellent color effects in your finished work, although great care must be used in this process.

Cementing

Plastic on Plastic

It is best to purchase one of the commercial solvent cements suited to the type of plastic you are using. They contain ingredients such as ethylene dichloride and chloroform, both of which dissolve the plastic. Experiment with scrap pieces, following the directions on the package for best results. Chloroform alone can be used as a cement, but highly volatile it is poisonous and dangerous to work with, especially for children, and is not recommended.

There are several methods of cementing plastics together:

Brushing

If you are going to join two flat pieces together, lay them down next to each other on a table and brush them with cement. After about five minutes press the pieces together. Do not press down too heavily. Remember that the cement softens the top surface, but unlike mortar, it does not fill any depressions, therefore the top surfaces will fit flush.

Soaking

This is the preferred method to use when a small piece is to be fastened to a large one: Pour a little cement in a dish. Lay the piece in it and let it stand at least one minute (larger pieces will require five minutes), until the surface has become soft. Place a few pins or tacks under the piece so that only one surface is softened while the other is raised out of the cement bath. Remove the excess cement and place the pieces together. A light pressure is all that is necessary.

If you are working with large pieces, this method is impractical; you must use the previous method of brushing on the cement.

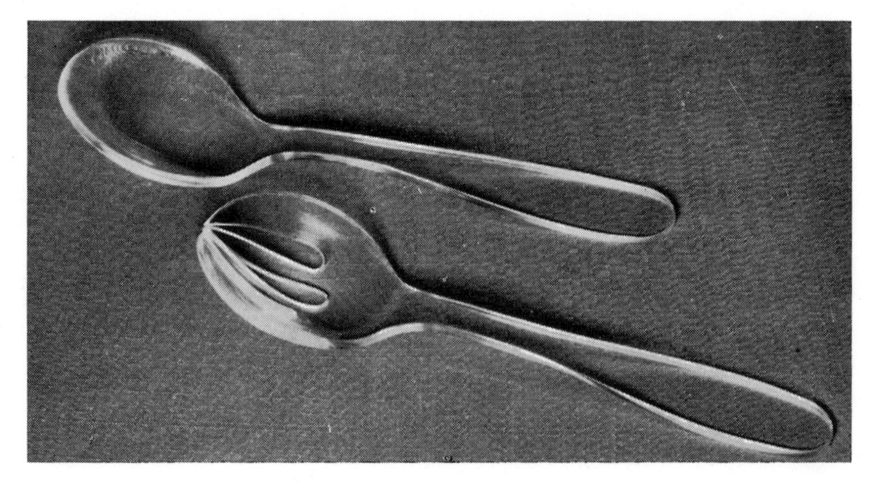

Pressed and slotted spoons (see illustration, opposite).

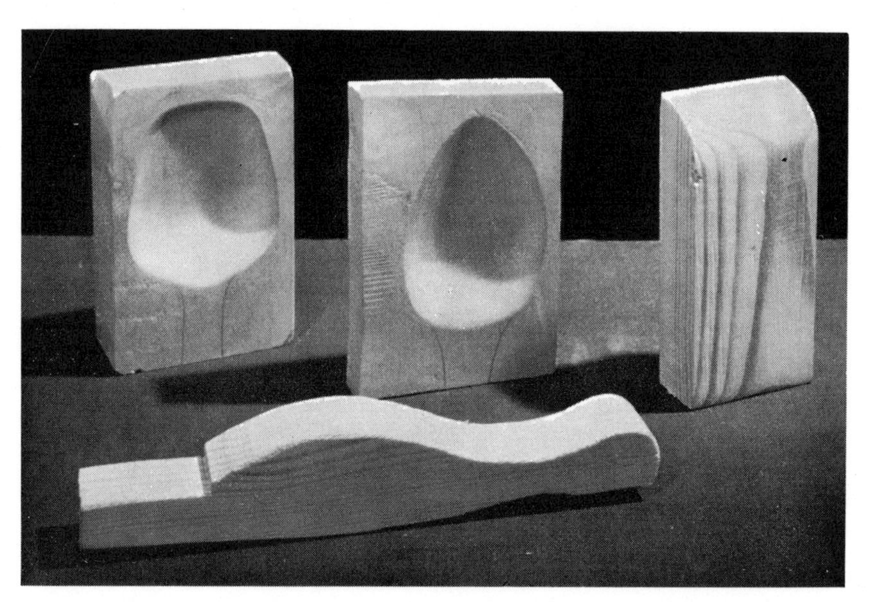

Top: Hollowed wooden forms are used for making plastic spoons.

Bottom: The cut out, warmed plastic is being pressed into the form; a glove is worn for protection as the plastic retains heat.

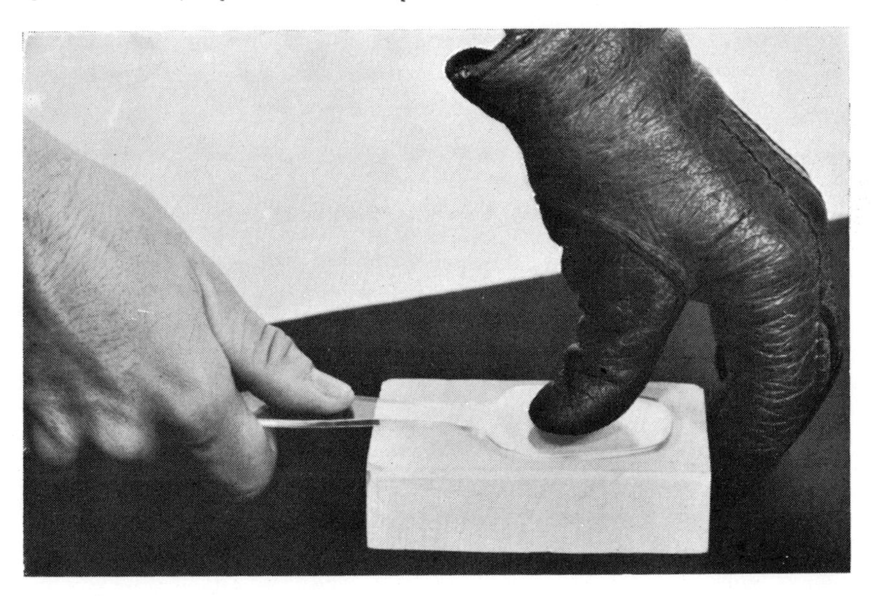

Cementing Plastics to Other Materials

You will need a cement that will both soften the plastic yet adhere to other materials, thin wood, metal, cork, paper, etc., so that these will, in turn, stick to the plastic. Cemented objects should dry for 24 hours. Hobby stores will be able to supply these special cements when you stipulate the materials you plan to join together.

Forming

Plastic can be twisted, bent, pressed, or blown into almost every possible shape. Warm the plastic first in a slightly warm kitchen oven (about 167° F.) until it becomes as soft as rubber. The plastic should be placed on a piece of asbestos or if it is a very small piece, on a cookie sheet. Templates and smoothly polished wooden molds are used for forming the plastic but a glass or bottle serves just as well.

Always use protective gloves when handling heated plastic. Lay the warmed plastic over the form or mold and form it until it begins to cool and stiffen. If the shape is not right the first time, the piece can be warmed again and again until the desired result is obtained.

A hot-plate or gas flame can also be used to heat pieces that are to be twisted or bent. Plastic does not conduct heat as does metal, so you can hold one end of the piece in your hand while working on the other end. Of course, you must not touch the heated part of the plastic without gloves as it does retain the heat!

DESIGNS IN PLASTIC

Key Rings and Luggage Tags

The metal chains and initials for these key rings and luggage tags can be purchased at hardware stores, in hobby shops, or from jewelry findings suppliers. A name and address can be engraved or scratched on the personalized tag. The triangular form is intended to hold car keys and is handily used as a windshield scraper. The luggage tag is made of two layers joined at both inner surfaces of a thin plastic (see dotted lines) on three sides, leaving the slotted end open to insert an address card.

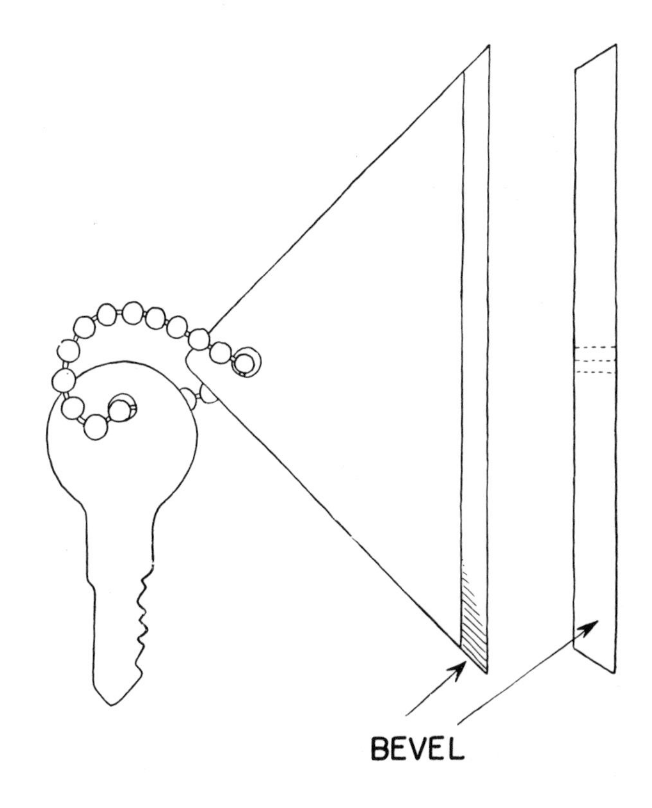

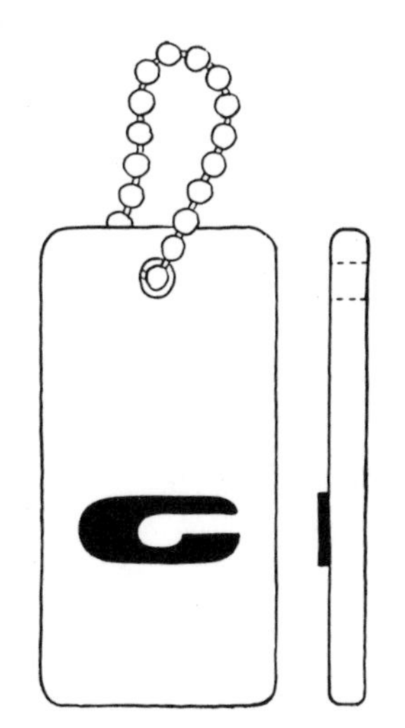

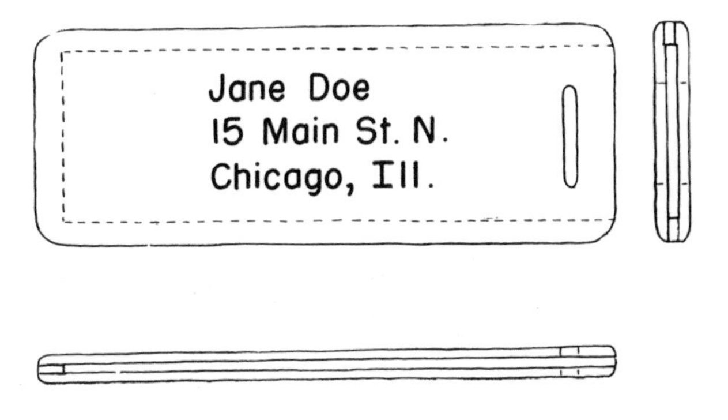

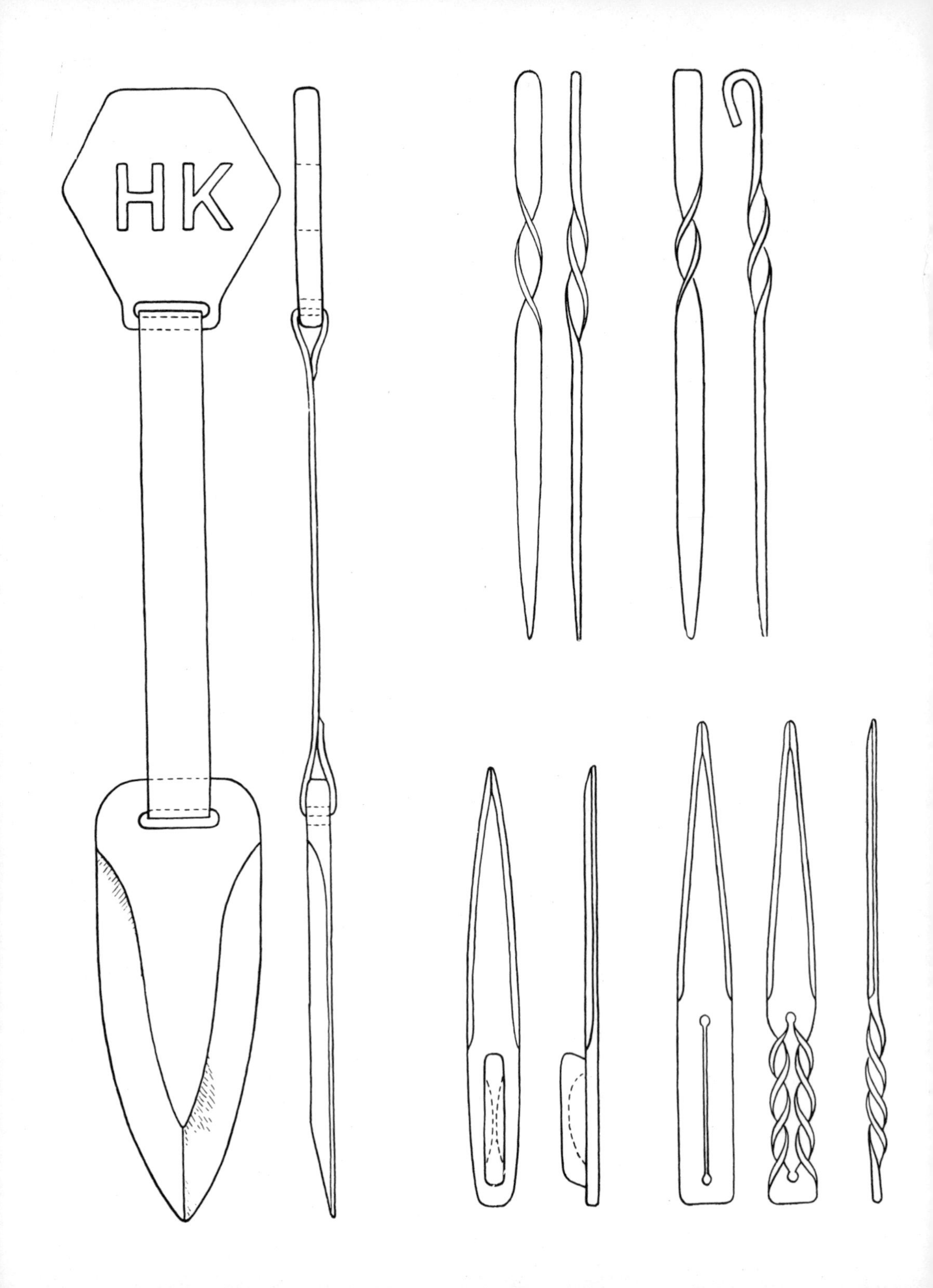
HK

See directions, next page.

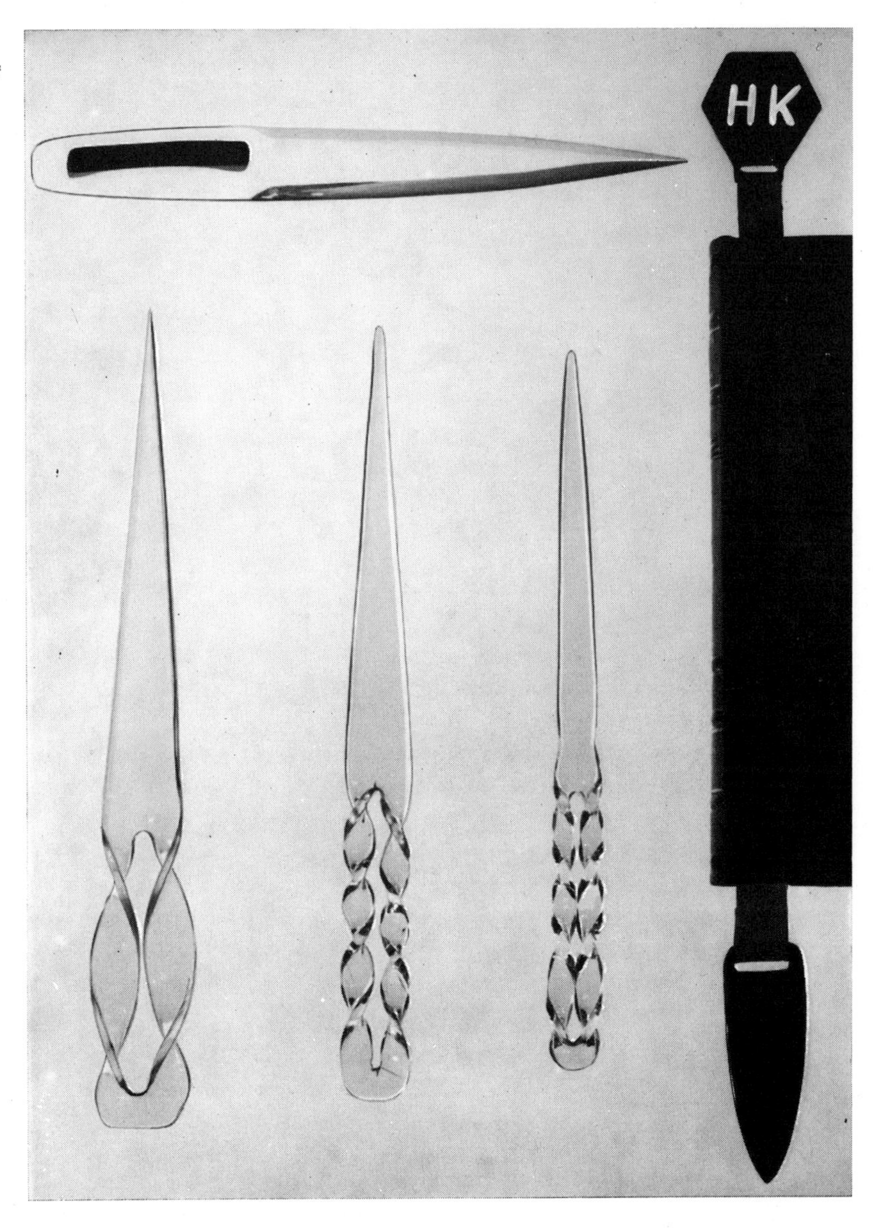

Letter Openers and Bookmarks

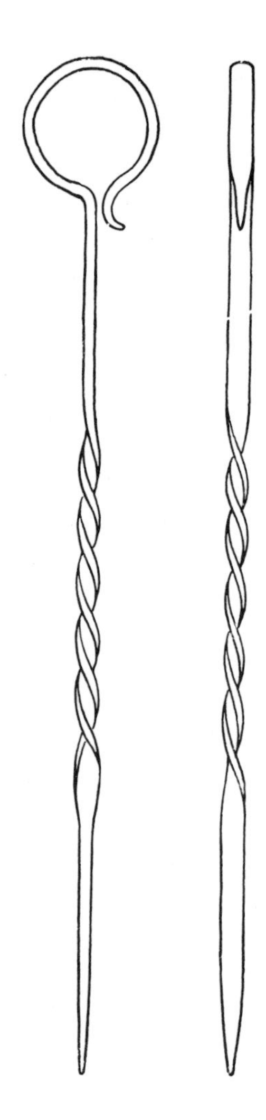

Spiraled Letter Opener (page 24)

Draw the pattern for the double-spiraled letter opener on a piece of paper as shown in the center drawing on the lower-right section of page 24. Drill the two holes and saw around the outline and through the opening slot. Twist as follows: Warm the handle area and insert the bottommost end of the handle up through the slot, once, twice, or three times as desired, and then pull and stretch it out evenly so that both sides match.

Flower Stake

The possibilities for variation in size and design here are endless. After warming the rod, twist this plant support into the desired design, then hold it straight for a moment until the plastic has stiffened.

Towel Rack

This is a handsome rack for hand towels, dish towels, and guest towels. Drill a hole within line *A* for inserting the saw blade, and two holes at marks *B* for mounting the towel rack to the wall. Widen the top of these last two holes so the screws may be countersunk. You can personalize the towel rack with the engraved names of members of the family, or mark it for guests. A long, modern flat towel rack may be made by simply bending the length forward leaving two flat ends for brackets, to be screwed to the wall through *two* vertical holes in each end since it will need more support.

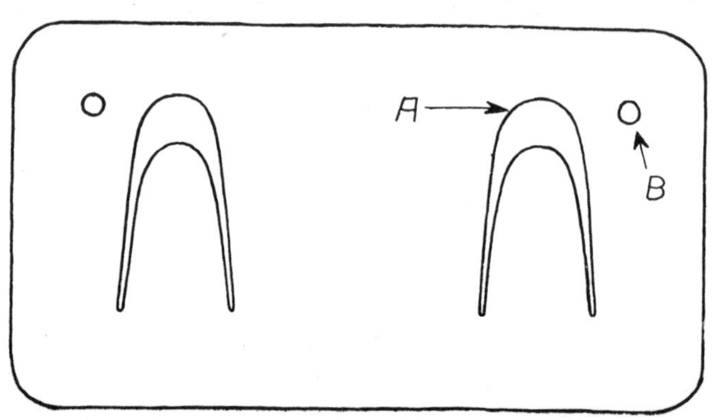

Towel Rack and Flower Stake

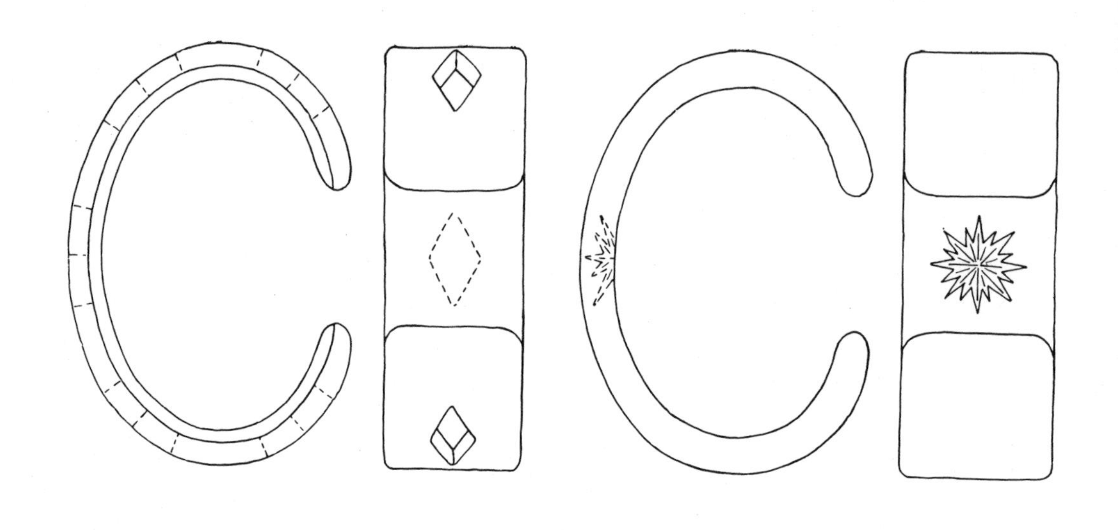

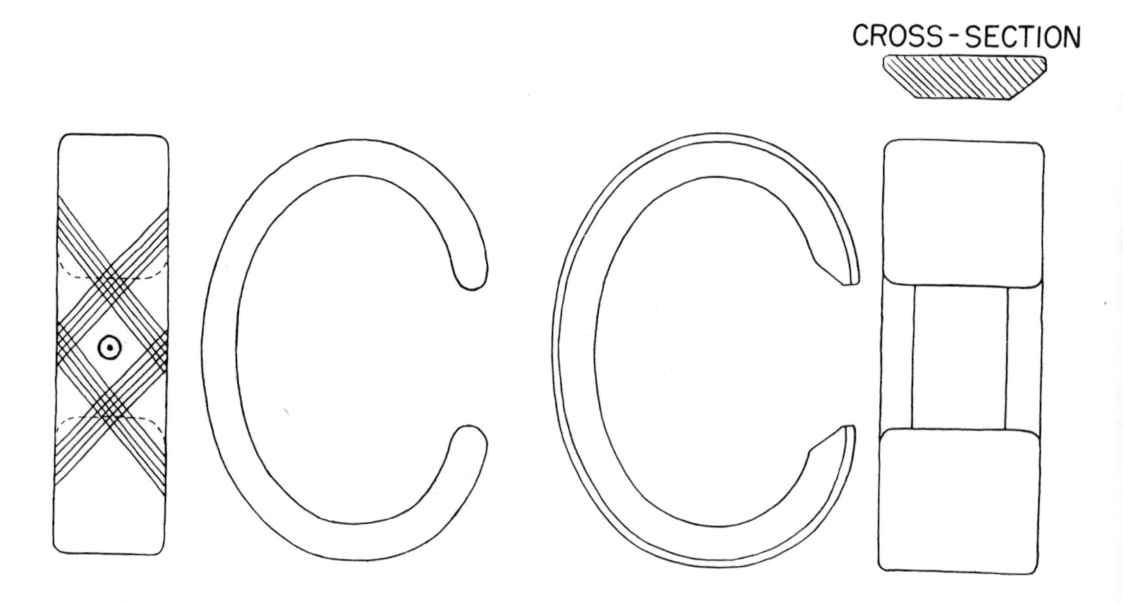
CROSS-SECTION

Bracelets are bent into shape after warming the plastic. They can be formed over a round piece of wood, a bottle, or the like. Note the profile of the bracelet that is lying on the table. It was given a little pressure at the center to make it convex while it was at the same time being formed over a mold. Decorations must be made before the bracelet is curved. The examples shown here include designs that are carved out of the top surface, or engraved—cut in—from the underside. Inlay work also makes handsome jewelry decoration.

Bracelets

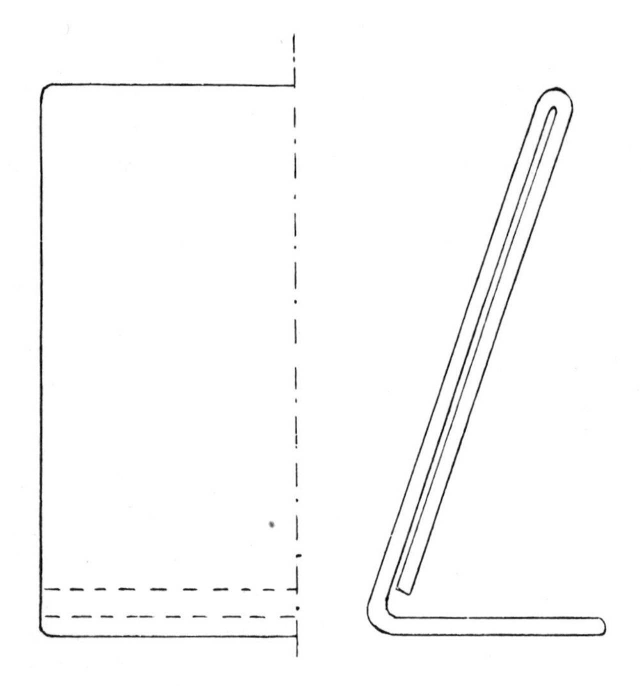

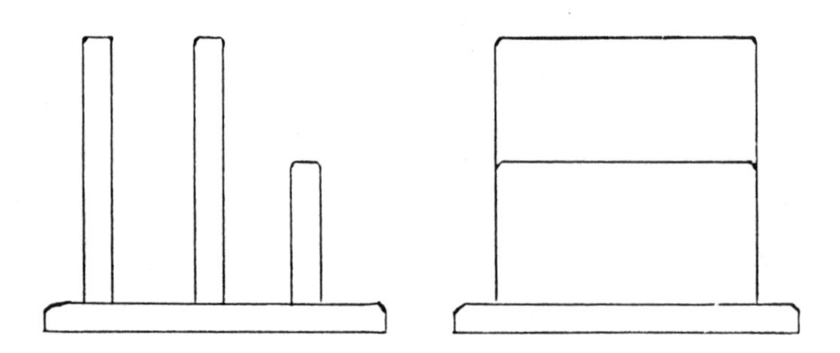

The frame is made just a little larger than the width of the photograph you will be using, and 2½ times the height of the picture to allow enough support after bending the plastic into shape. The picture frame is made simply by bending it as shown in the diagram opposite. The letter stand is made by cementing flat pieces of plastic to a beveled base (see cementing, p. 19).

Picture Frame and Letter Stand

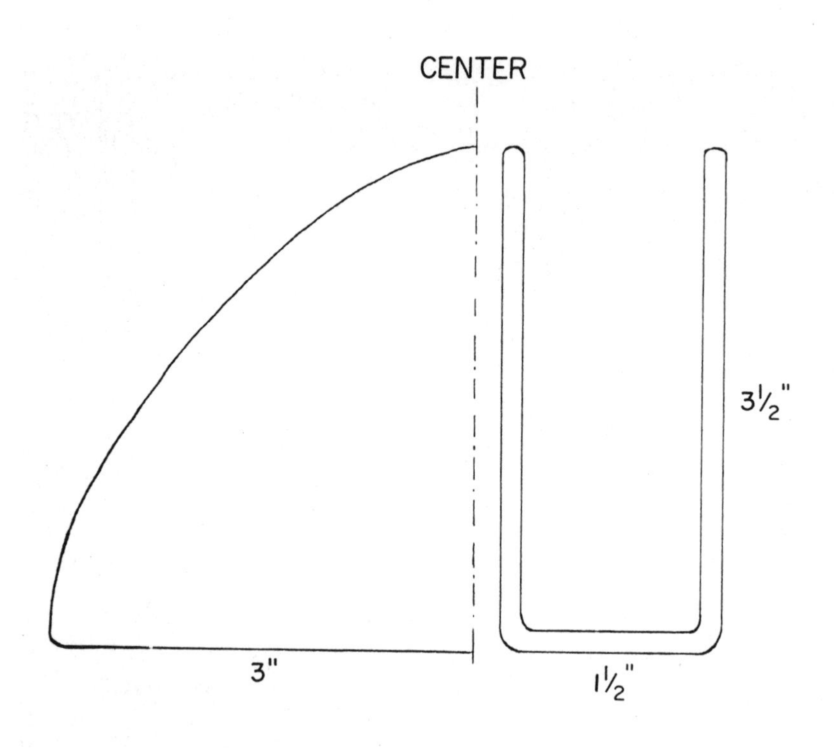
CENTER
3"
3½"
1½"

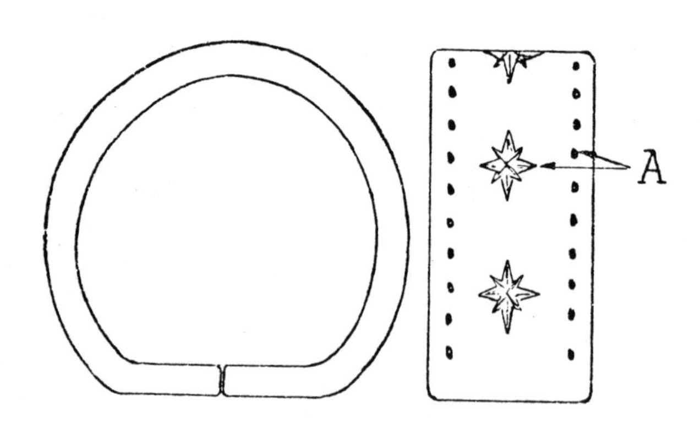
A

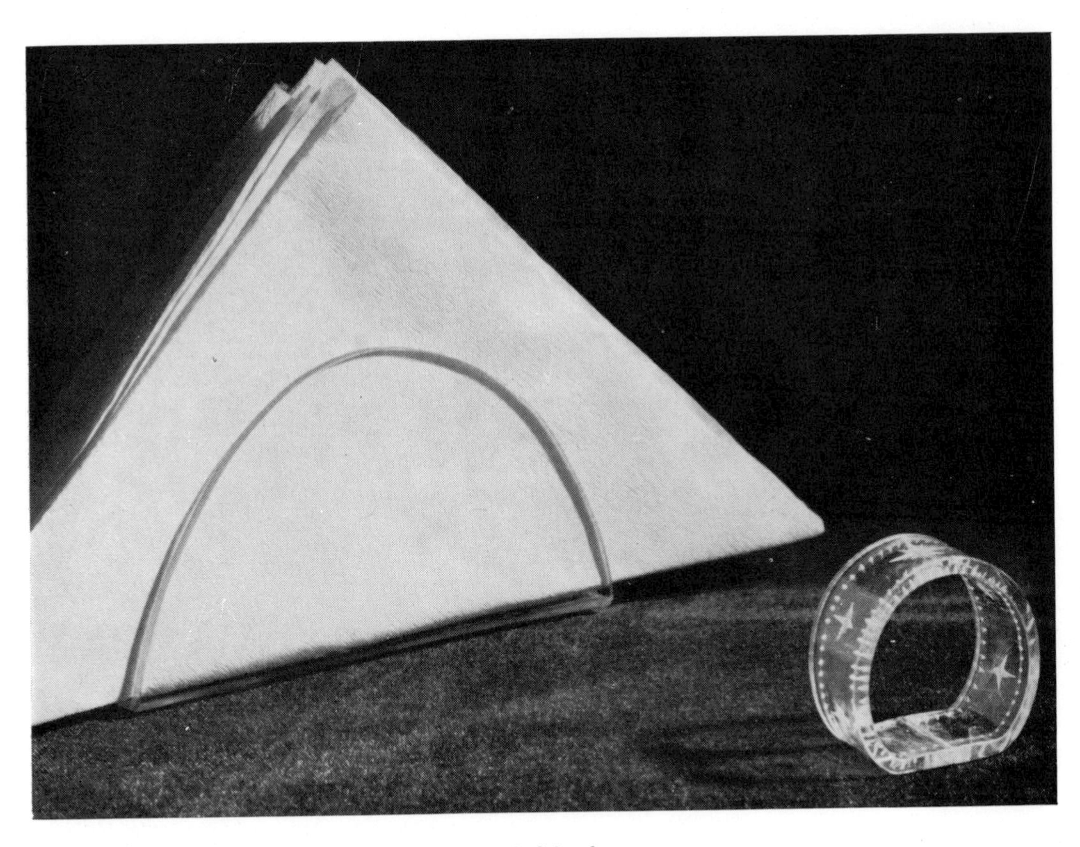

The napkin ring may be decorated or initialed in the same manner as the bracelets (p. 29). Here it has been decorated as in *A* with holes drilled partway through from within while stars were engraved on the outer surface. The lower drawing shows the profile of the napkin ring formed from a 5½″ plastic piece. The stand is formed by bending a 6″ x 8½″ plastic slab as shown, after the curve has been cut at both ends.

Napkin Stand and Napkin Ring

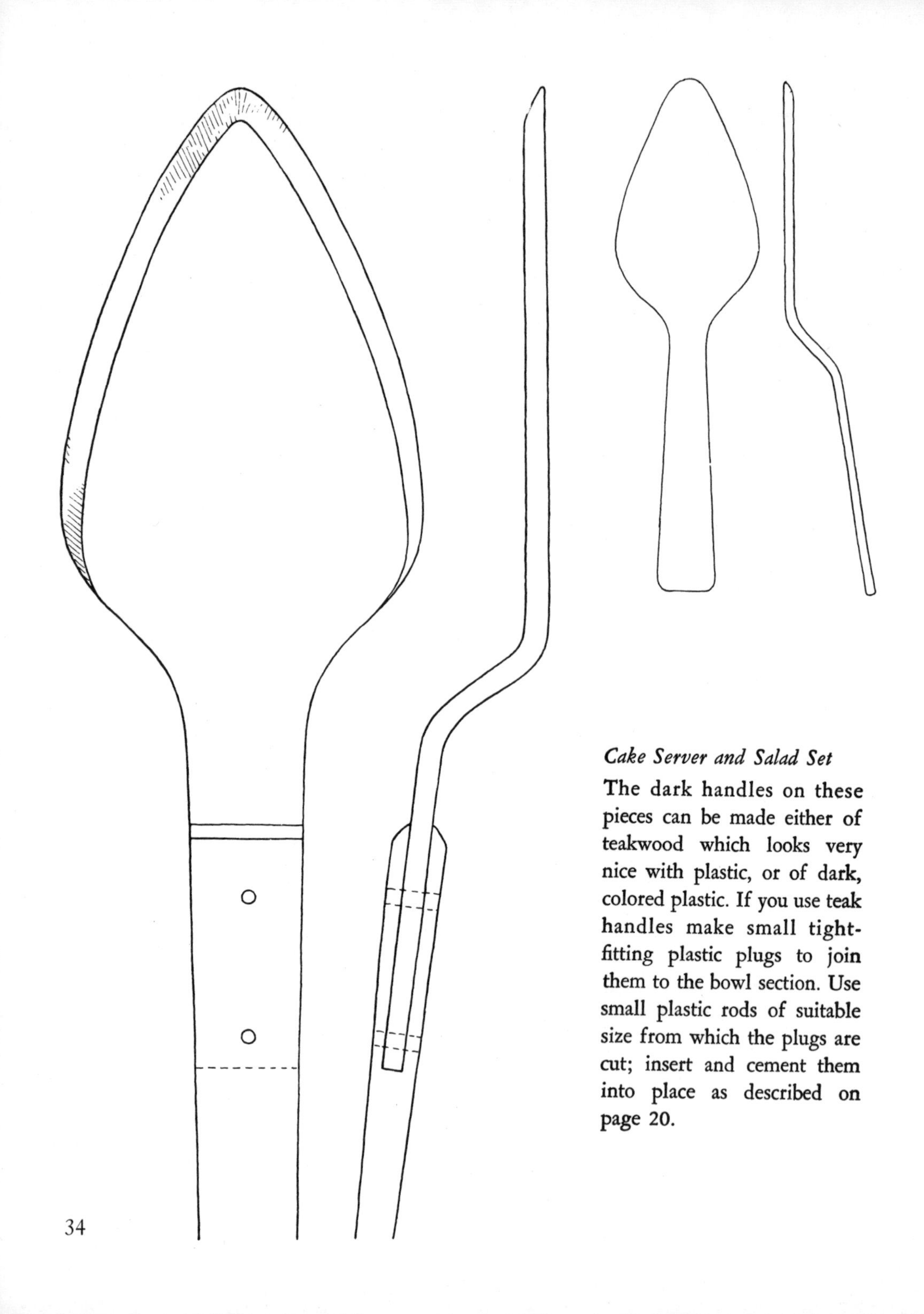

Cake Server and Salad Set

The dark handles on these pieces can be made either of teakwood which looks very nice with plastic, or of dark, colored plastic. If you use teak handles make small tight-fitting plastic plugs to join them to the bowl section. Use small plastic rods of suitable size from which the plugs are cut; insert and cement them into place as described on page 20.

See diagrams, opposite.

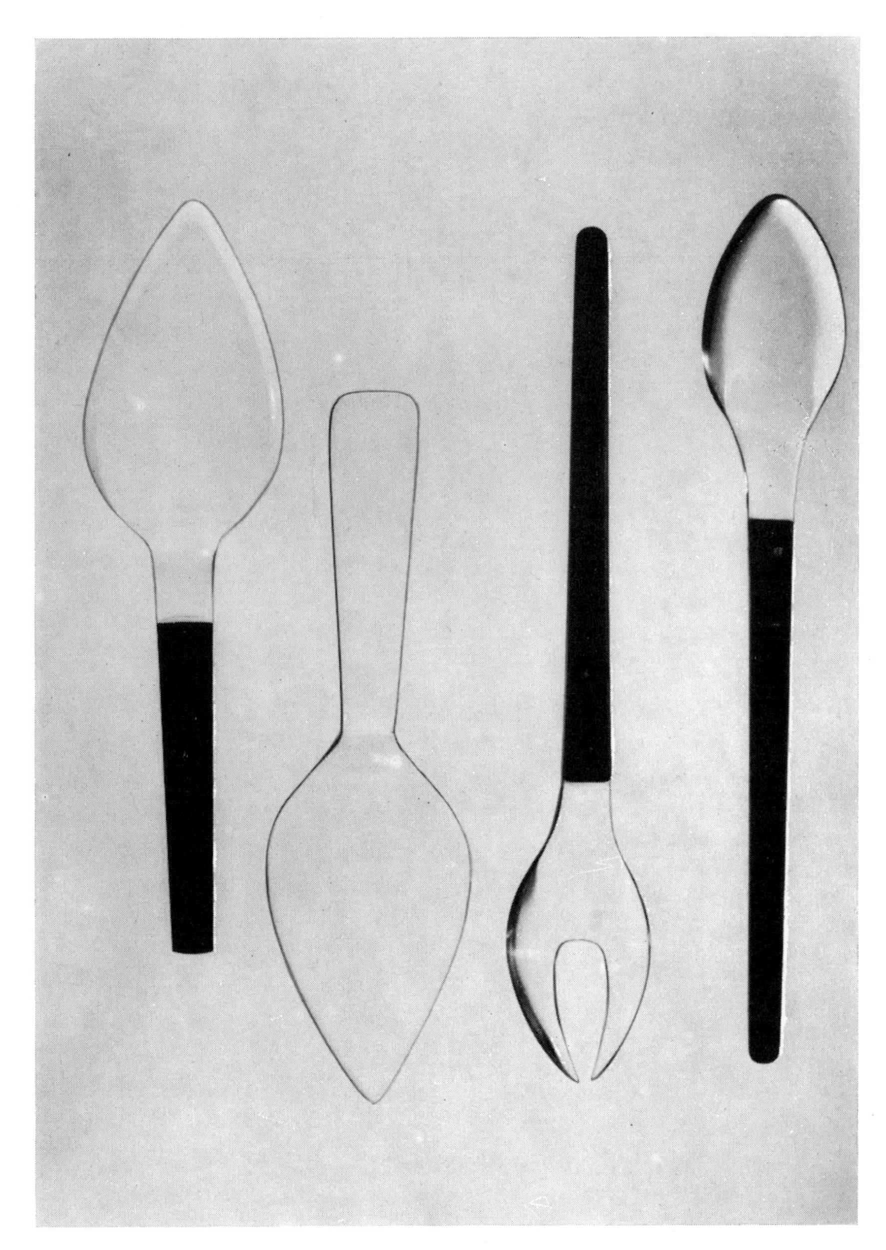

Cake Servers and Salad Set

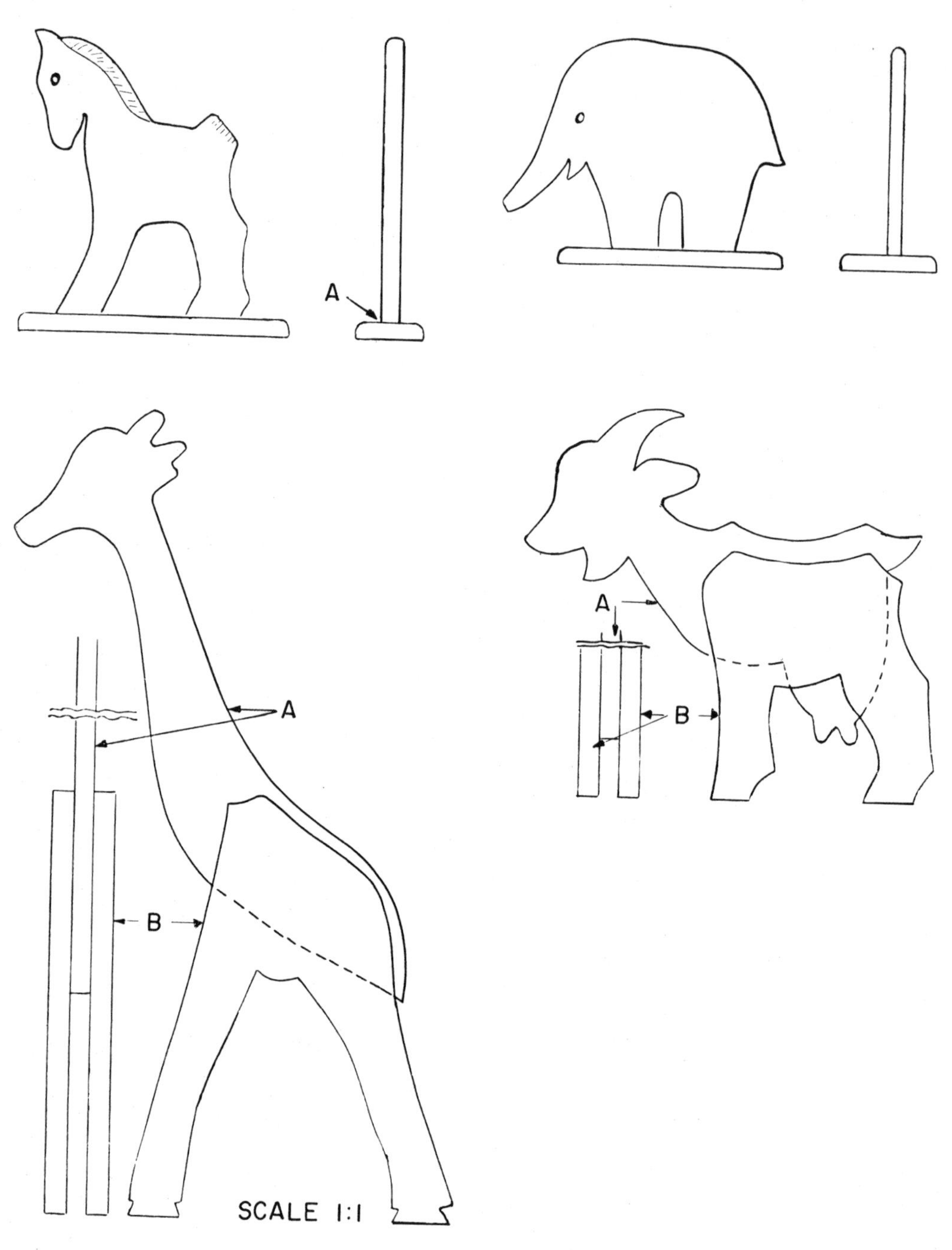
A
A
B
A
B
SCALE 1:1

These animals are sawed from plastic sheets and separate parts are joined with brads so they may easily be taken apart. They are fine manipulative toys for young children who enjoy taking them apart and putting them together again. The animals can also be taken apart and by tracing around the pieces as patterns, many more animals can be cut out of paper and colored with crayons. The single piece toys can be cemented to a small rectangular stand.

Toy Animals

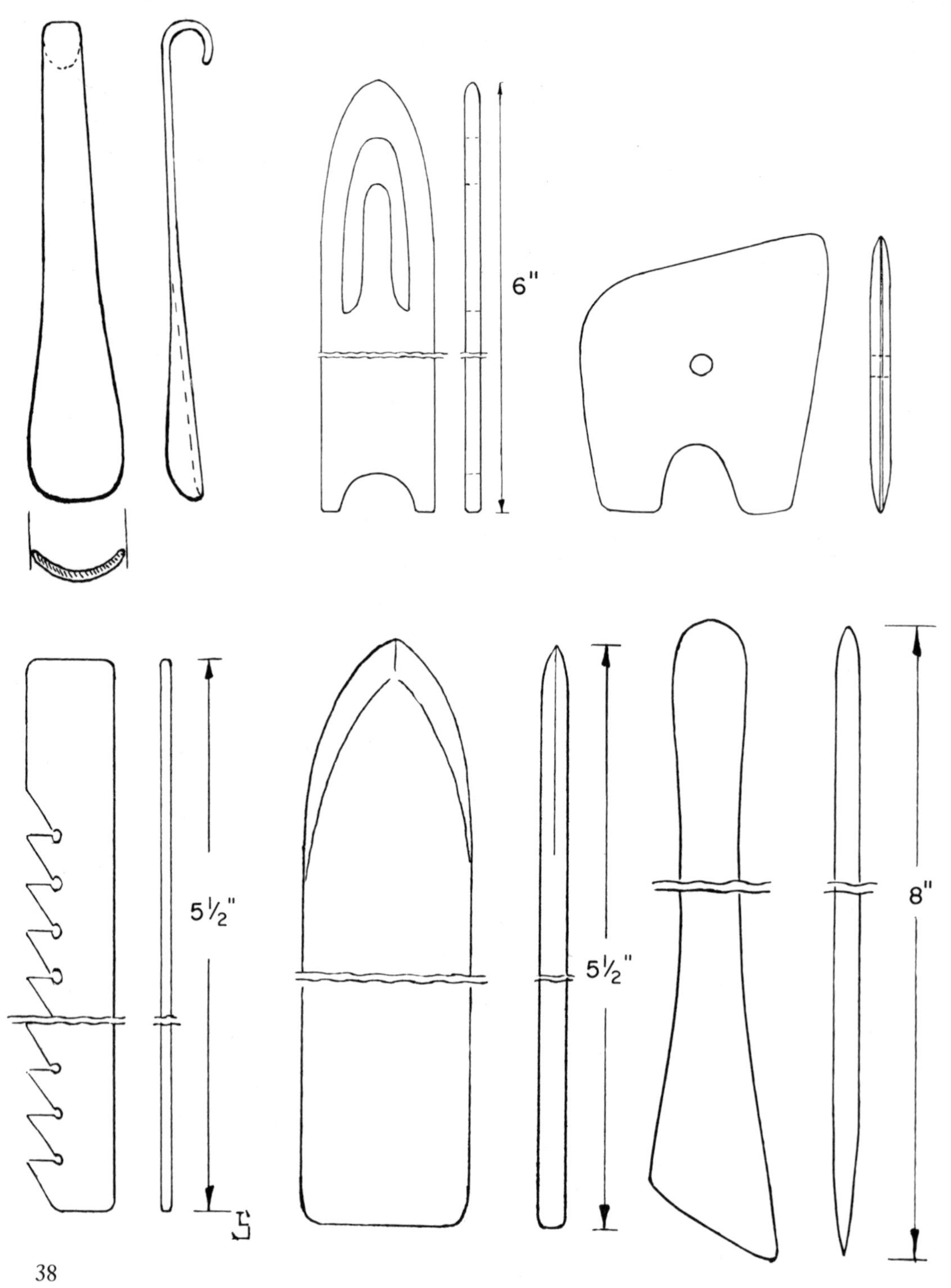
6"
5½"
5½"
8"

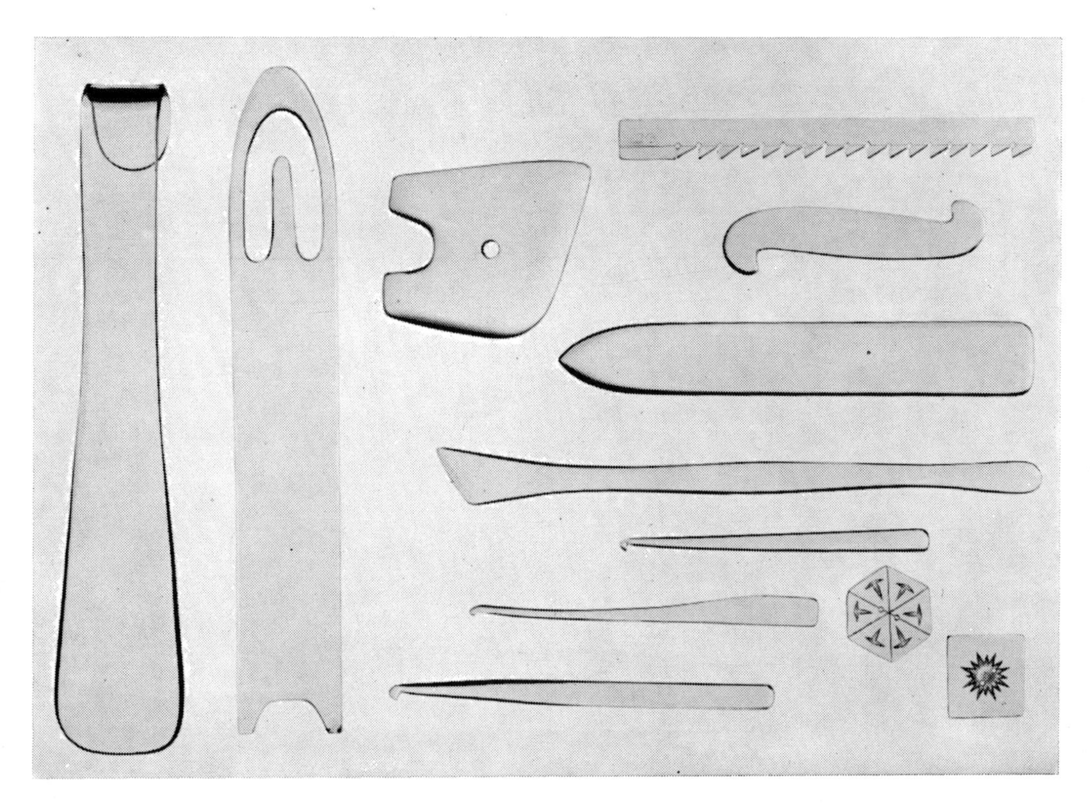

In the drawing on page 38 are shown: a shoehorn, a netting needle for making or repairing fish nets; string bags; or decorative hangings, a weaving shuttle, a scraper for clay modeling, a hole punch guide for preparing leather for stitching, and—at the lower right—several other clay-modeling tools. In the photograph above are a crochet hook and buttons which can also be attached to cuff-link backs, available at hobby shops.

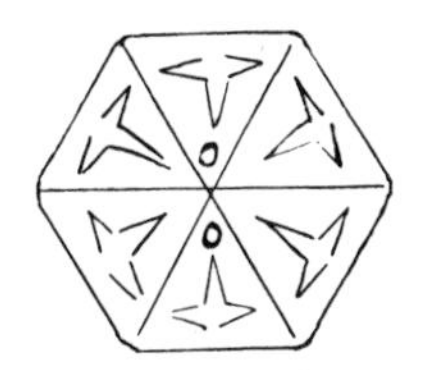

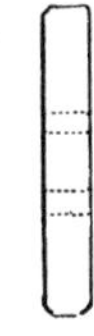

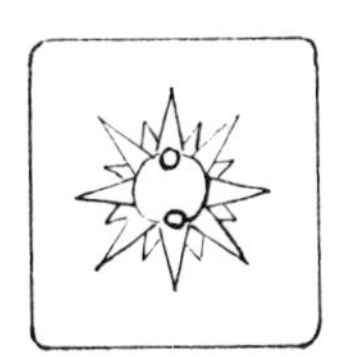

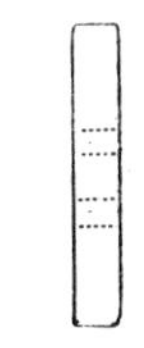

Plastic Tools for Craftwork

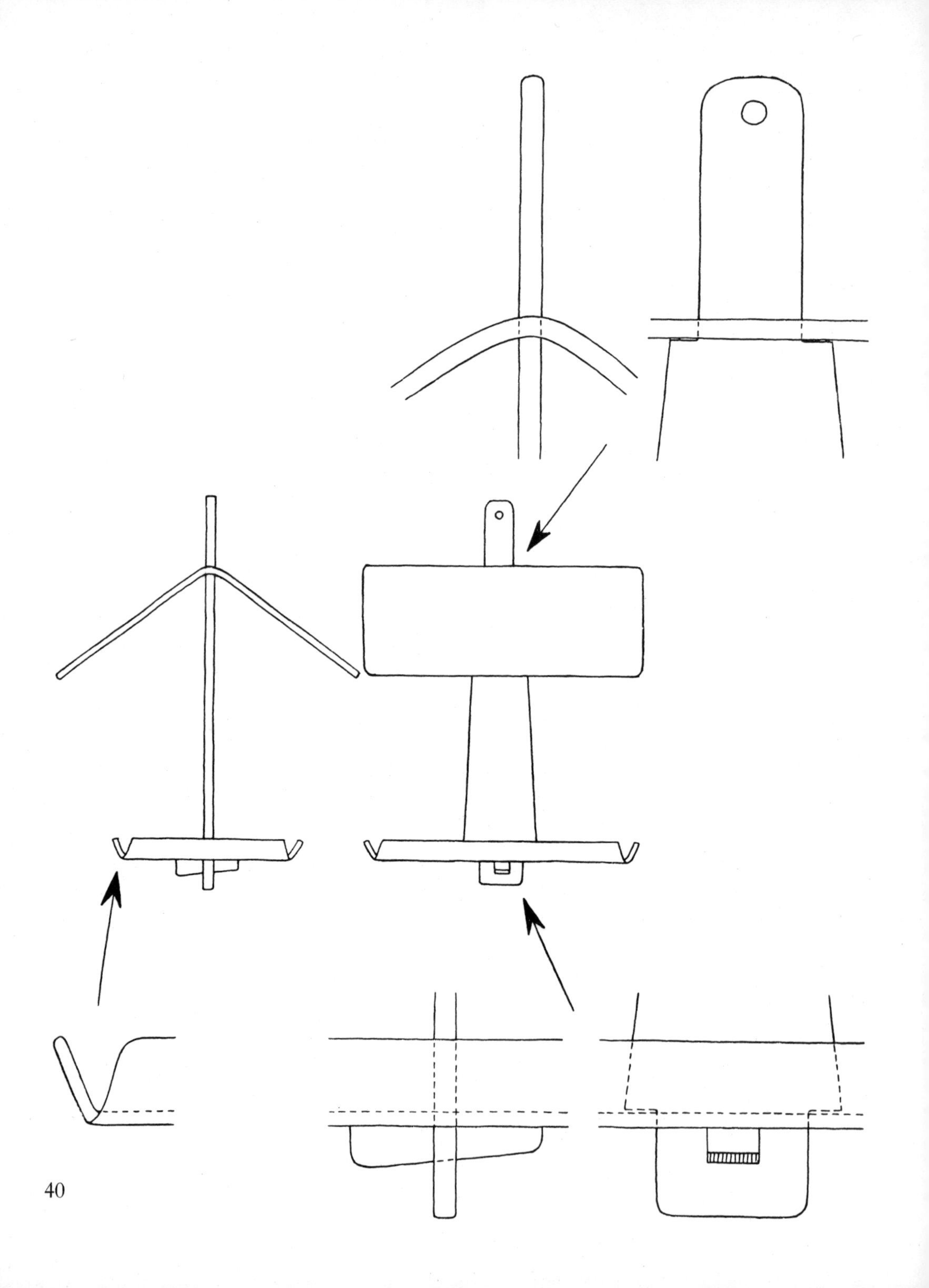

Bird lovers can let their imaginations go in adapting the design of this bird-feeder. This one is intended to be hung, but the wedge which holds the feeder base can be lengthened so that the feeder may be rigidly attached to a wall.

Bird-Feeder

This hanger is excellent for travel as it can be folded small and since it does not absorb water it is easily wiped dry for repacking, after doing light laundry. The hook is removed from a wooden hanger and can be re-used here.

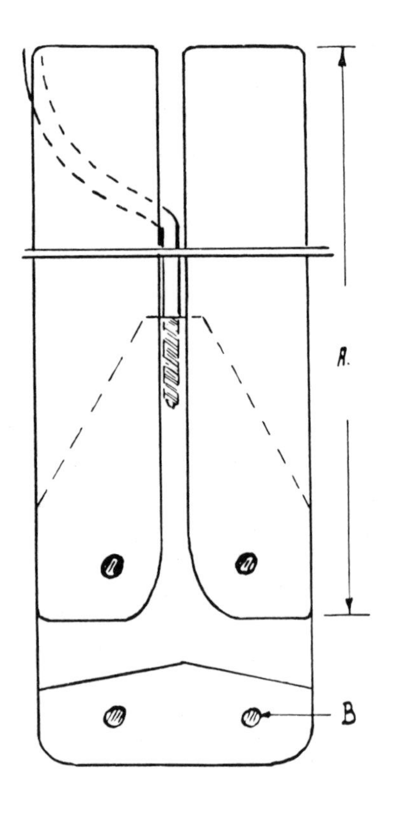

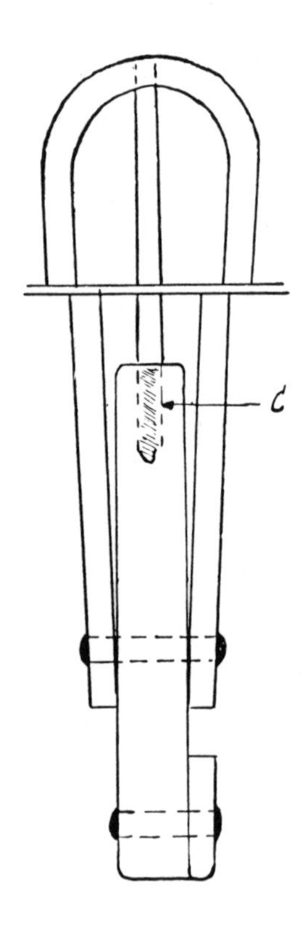

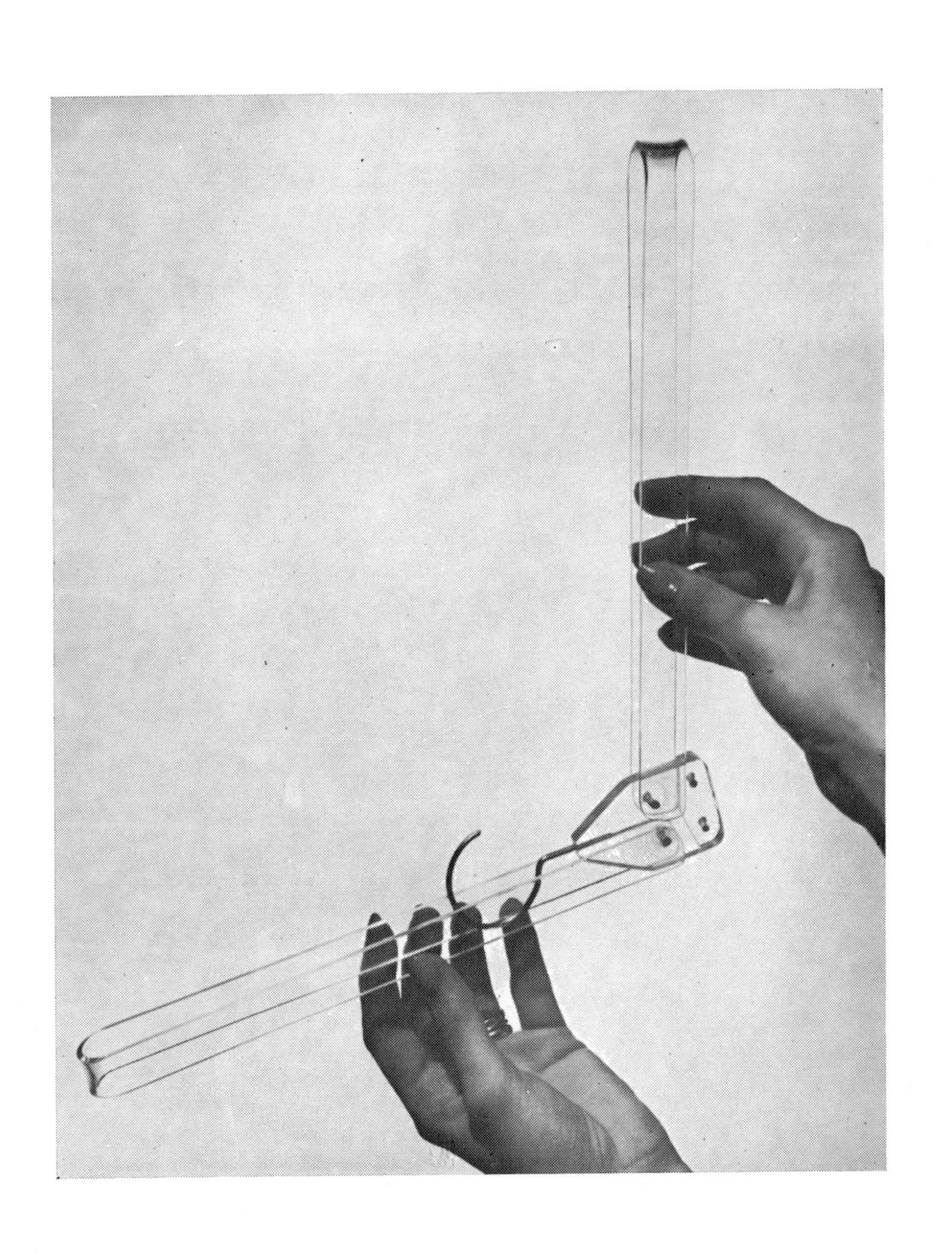

Folding Travel Hanger

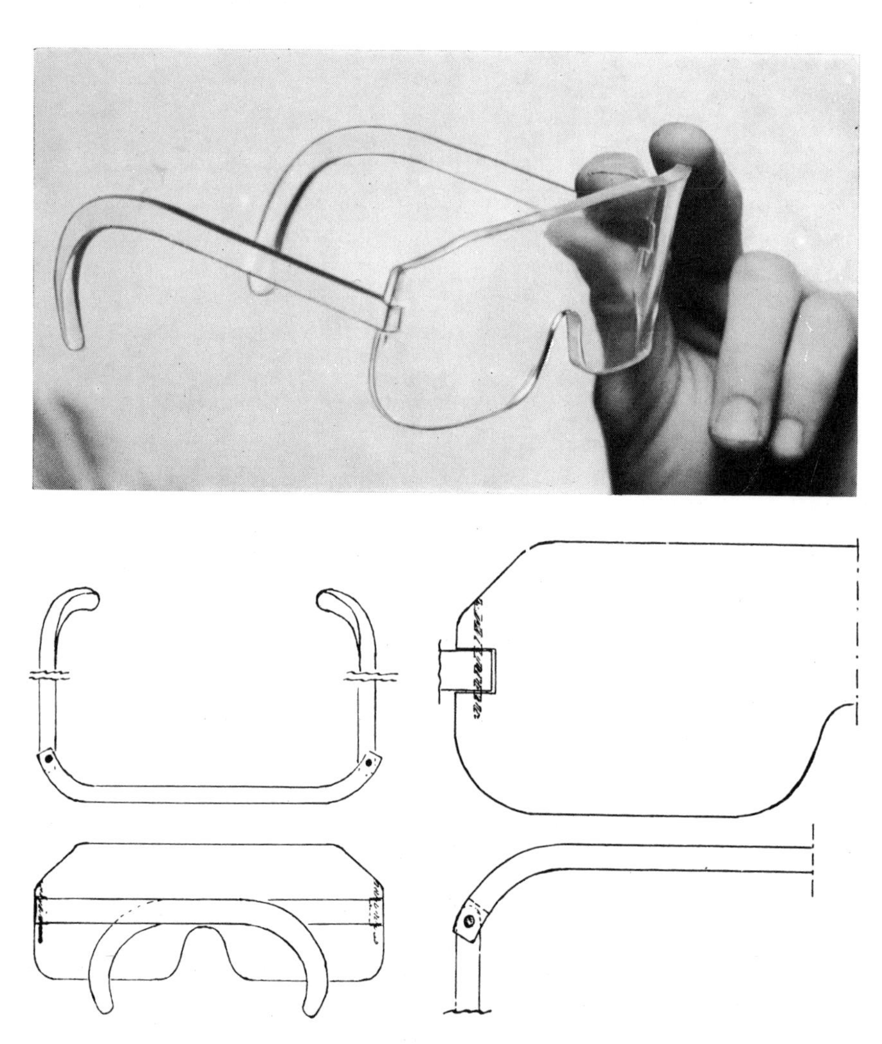

This is a very helpful accessory for anyone working with large power tools. It is easy to make and should be beveled to fit your nose comfortably. Made of tinted plastic it also serves as a fine sun shield.

Protective Eye Shield

Clear Polyester Casting Resin

Working with this material is quite different from working with acrylic plastic, but it offers many further creative possibilities. It is not difficult to use, particularly when working on small projects. The only precaution that you absolutely must be sure to take when working indoors, is to have very good ventilation as the vapor from these volatile chemicals is harmful. Also, be very careful not to get any of the catalyst or the hardener in your eyes as it is very corrosive.

The two principal methods of using polyester casting resin are:

1. *Casting and embedment.*
2. *Reinforcing with fiber glass.*

General directions for these techniques are given on the following pages together with some design ideas which should prove helpful to hobbyists working with this new plastic.

Embedment with Polyester Casting Resin

Polyester casting resin makes it possible to embed all sorts of decorative objects in clear plastic. With very little difficulty you can make extremely naturalistic jewelry, paperweights, or specimen samples for collecting, teaching aids, etc.

What can be embedded in plastic?

Almost anything. Plants, dried insects and colorful butterflies, snail shells, rocks, miniature models, photographs, identity cards, etc., all are well-suited to embedment. Flowers and colorful leaves may also be embedded and preserved. The possibilities are endless. It is easier to embed objects when they are dry, thus flowers should be pressed in paper toweling and kept for a week before you attempt to embed them.

The casting process is much like making a fancy gelatin fruit mold where the fruit is positioned at a certain level. First a gelatin base is made and allowed to solidify, then the fruit is arranged on this and the rest of the gelatin is poured over it. Do the same with plastic.

A general description for the use of polyester casting resin, which is available at most hobby shops, follows.

Chemical Hardeners

Clear polyester casting resin comes in pint, quart, or gallon containers for hobby use. You must also buy a catalyst or hardener which is added to the plastic to harden it. This may, in some cases, be attached to the resin can and sold as a unit.

Tools

You will need a cup, glass, or porcelain bowl for mixing the plastic. (Small portions can be mixed in a paper bag.) Teaspoons, tablespoons, and a cup are needed plus an eye dropper for the hardener. Use wooden sticks for stirring. Glass or polished metal molds are good but wood and lead with smoothly polished surfaces can also be used for molds. If you want to make a plastic copy of an object you already have, plaster of Paris can be used in making the mold.

If the mold is not made of too many pieces, you can grease it to remove the molded plastic more easily without spoiling the mold. (Placing the mold in water just below boiling for 10 minutes—then in cold water for 10 minutes more—is another means of removing the plastic from the mold.)

Preheat the plastic on a slightly warmed hotplate or in warm water then place it in a warm, not hot, oven. Incandescent and sun lamps can also be used for preheating. Artificial heat is not really necessary, but it speeds up the hardening process. The plastic will harden at room temperatures of about 70° F., but not at less than 66° F.

Procedure

Make sure that the pieces to be embedded are dry and clean. You must also check the mold to see that the surface is completely clean and smooth. Be sure that the mold is a suitable size for the project as the object to be embedded must be completely covered with plastic. Remember to grease the interior surface of the mold with paste wax or margarine to make it easier to get the molded piece out of the form.

Mix a sufficient quantity of the plastic and hardener to make the base of the piece. Do not, however, mix more than you can use in 10 to 15 minutes. Follow the manufacturer's specific instructions on the plastic container. In general, more hardener is needed if the temperature is under 70° F. and less hardener is to be added if the room temperature is higher. At 70° F. use about 10 drops of hardener per ounce of resin for small projects and 5 drops per ounce for larger items (paperweights, etc.). Stir the mixture with a

stick for about 30 seconds to remove all the air bubbles! Pour the mixture into the mold and let the mass harden for a few minutes more.

Place the object to be embedded in the desired position on this plastic base.

Mix another batch of plastic and hardener in sufficient quantity to completely cover the entire object, then carefully pour the plastic over the object so that all the corners and cavities are filled and air bubbles are avoided. Work slowly and gradually. If the package directions suggest it, place the form in a warm place until the plastic hardens, but be careful not to get the heat too high or the plastic will crack. Small projects will harden in 25-30 minutes.

These are some suggestions for warming plastic: 1. Place the form in a saucepan of warm water which is kept just below the boiling point. 2. The electric or gas oven is a good heat source but do not put the form directly in contact with the bottom of the oven. 3. Place the form on a hotplate, an electric heater, or on a sunny windowsill. 4. The heat from a light bulb will be sufficient for small objects.

Artificial heat introduced during hardening is not necessary, but it does speed up the process. This plastic will harden at normal room temperature (72° F.) after ½ to 1½ hours, but it won't be completely hard for from 8 to 14 days. It is important to remember this when working on large pieces. Cracking can be prevented, particularly on the thick pieces (⅜"-4"), by adding a smaller proportion of hardener. For the largest pieces 1/50 of the normal amount of hardener can be used, but this will extend the initial hardening time to about two days.

The hardening process itself generates heat, which can become quite intense in large pieces.

When the plastic has hardened, place the form to one side and allow it to cool slowly. After cooling, remove the hardened plastic from the mold. If it is completely smooth, further sanding and polishing is not necessary. But if there is a small flaw (a finger mark shows very clearly) the surface should be sanded as described in the section on acrylic plastic.

Transparent plastic is the preferred material for these projects, but colored plastic is also excellent, particularly in obtaining certain contrast effects. This offers a rich field for experimentation.

Coloring Polyester Casting Resin

Coloring polyester casting resin is quite a different process than coloring acrylic plastic and the results are much nicer. The colors are added before the hardener. Special dyes and pigments have been developed for this purpose and are available in hobby shops which carry the casting resin.

Opaque colors: Pigments in paste form are used to color the plastic. A drop or two on the end of a toothpick is all that is needed to color an ounce of resin. Too much pigment will slow down the hardening process.

Transparent colors: Liquid dye for use on casting resin is available in hobby shops. It is used for obtaining a clear transparent color. Use only a drop or two of the coloring per ounce of resin.

In both methods it is important to mix in the dye very carefully. If air bubbles form, let the mass stand until they have disappeared.

Fiber Glass Reinforcement for Plastics

In reinforcing plastic use fiber-glass cloth. Fiber glass is made by smelting a special kind of alkali-free glass which can be drawn into very thin hairlike threads. These threads are woven together so that they lie in both directions. When this is embedded in plastic resin it stabilizes it immensely.

Either fiber-glass cloth or coarser fiber-glass mats may be used. The first is good for working with thin objects, and the latter is better for heavier pieces. In building up very heavy sheets use several layers of fiber glass. Two layers of fiber-glass cloth with a layer of fiber-glass mat in the middle may be used, or there could even be more layers, depending upon the project and its requirements.

Reinforcement procedure:

Arrange a layer of plastic resin in the mold with a brush or spray gun. While the plastic is still damp, place a layer of fiber glass on it, followed by another layer of plastic resin, and continue this alternate layering until you have as many fiber-glass layers as you need. End with a final layer of the resin. Make sure that the resin thoroughly penetrates the spaces between the woven glass fibers in each layer.

When the plastic has hardened it can, if necessary, be treated with epoxy putty, then sanded, wet buffed, and polished or painted.

In making thinner reinforced sheets it is a good idea immediately after spreading the last layer, to lay a thick sheet of glazed paper over it and go over this with a ruler, pressing down hard and scraping off the excess plastic, working from the center outward to the sides. This also helps to eliminate any air bubbles.

Suggested Projects in Reinforced Plastic:

Windowpanes for entrances, bathrooms, kitchens, upper portions of balconies, and light-diffusing frames.

Sun blinds or "glass" roofs over porches, garden patios, etc. in colors.

Tops for picnic or game tables.

For any of these projects use glass, polished wood, or metal as a base for your mold, cut to the desired size and shape. Spread the mold with a layer of paste wax or margarine as mentioned earlier. Lay on the plastic resin and fiber glass in one or more layers as described above. Finally, even out the top surface of the plastic with a sheet of glazed paper and go over it with a ruler. Colored plastic in pale tones, such as sea-green, have a handsome effect because of the glass threads which make a textured pattern in the plastic and break up the color.

Wall plaques for children's rooms and play areas or *panels* to be inserted in a crib can be made in this way: Spread plastic on a waxed, flat surface. On top of this lay the desired picture (design, chart, photograph, time schedules, etc.) with the picture side down. Spread another thin layer of the plastic resin over this, then a layer of fiber-glass cloth, and a final layer of plastic. Spread it out evenly and clear away any excess.

Covering wood with reinforced plastic. An old wall, a leaky boat, etc. can be covered with plastic with particularly good results.

Procedure: Scrape the wood completely clean—getting rid of any old paint, tar, or dirt which will have accumulated. Sand the surface with coarse sandpaper so the plastic resin will grip and adhere to it. You should pre-cut the fiber-glass cloth into pieces which will fit the size and shape of the object or area to be covered and allow 3/4" to 1 1/4" for overlapping. Then proceed as described above. To remove excess plastic and air bubbles, use heavy paper and a ruler rubbed repeatedly over it from a central area to the outer edge.

In *re-covering a boat* the following points must be considered: The lasting quality of the job depends on how deeply the plastic resin penetrates into the wood. For this reason lacquer remover must *not* be used, because it hinders this plastic penetration. Nor should blowtorches be used to remove old paint because they will draw out oil from the paint and force it into the pores of the wood. Only if motor oil has penetrated through the bottom of the wood should the blowtorch be used—to drive the oil all the way through the wood to its outer surface, where it can then be removed with carbon tetrachloride or a strong lye.

It is essential that the boat be completely dried out for this work, and, incidentally, while you are working on it the boat should not be exposed to direct sunlight because it will make the plastic harden too rapidly, possibly causing it to crack. Copper or brass nails and screws should be countersunk and covered with plastic wood, which can also be used to fill small cracks and crevices.

The rest of the procedure is the same as described previously except that the first layer of plastic resin should be allowed to adequately penetrate the wood and harden. When it is quite hard, spread on another layer and lay on the fiber-glass cloth then cover it with the plastic resin. It is wise to mix the plastic resin in small portions as the work proceeds. Also remember to rinse the brush regularly in brush cleaner (acetone) so that the bristles do not become stiff.

The number of layers of fiber glass that should be used will depend upon the size and construction of the boat. As a general guide we suggest that one layer will be enough on small boats up to 16 feet in length. A boat that is 18 to 26 feet long will need two layers, and a 32- to 45-foot boat should have at least 3 or 4 layers. Fiber-glass cloth is available in 38″, 44″, and 60″ widths. Fiber-glass tape 4″ and 6″ wide is also available.

This treatment will make the boat completely watertight. It strengthens the boat and eliminates the porosity of the wood. It will not freeze, is acid-resistant, and impervious to the effects of salt water and sun. There will be no annual repairs and the expense involved is no more than the cost of an overhauling with ordinary boat lacquer. Furthermore, according to marine experts, the weight of this plastic coating is less than the water which the boat's sides and bottom would normally absorb.

Building Toy Car Bodies and Boats of Reinforced Plastic

Instead of a crude soap-box car boys can make a toy automobile or racing-car with an elegant plastic body that will not splinter or bulge! The mold can be made of fiber, plaster of Paris, and cardboard which has been treated with paste wax so that the plastic form can later be removed. Remember that there must be an opening in the mold and some method used, such as oiling or waxing the mold, to permit removal of the molded piece.

A boat can be made in the same manner, but, naturally, it is a bigger job. The mold could be an old, discarded, wooden boat, which must then have its surface perfected and prepared as you would any other mold. Or you could build a new mold of wood, plaster of Paris, or both in conjunction over a framework of wire mesh covered with burlap and smeared over with plaster of Paris. To prevent the plaster of Paris from setting too rapidly, it can be mixed with beer of less than ½% alcohol content—"Zing," made by the Kingsbury Brewing Co. is one brand available; "Jet," made by the U. S. Brewing Co. of Chicago, Ill., is another.

The seats can be made entirely of reinforced plastic and cemented with the same material. Air tanks can be cast in the bow and stern of the boat in the same way.

The plastic must be given adequate time to harden—at least two weeks—before floating the boat in the water. During the hardening period it is important that the temperature should at no time fall below 66°-68° F. in order to obtain proper results.

Bone - Man's Oldest Weapon

The first people who left us traces of their living habits were wandering hunters who moved to Northern Europe during the Early Stone Age. The best-preserved articles remaining of their culture are all pieces made of bone or reindeer antlers.

They eventually had become permanent settlers, and the objects made of bone which remain from this period are so numerous that one is almost tempted to call it the "Bone Age."

Axe-heads, flint flakers, fishing spears, and fish hooks have been found.

It is comforting to realize that man's desire for beauty was apparent even then, but the material they worked with was not so easy to handle. Look at the pointed axe in the photograph, for example. It was made from the bone of the European bison, or auroch, and its handsome ornamentation was almost certainly scratched in with a sharp piece of flint. The design motif was almost always a reflection of their daily tasks: from sewing, winding, and knotting, to chopping. Only rarely did they attempt to make representations of the human figure.

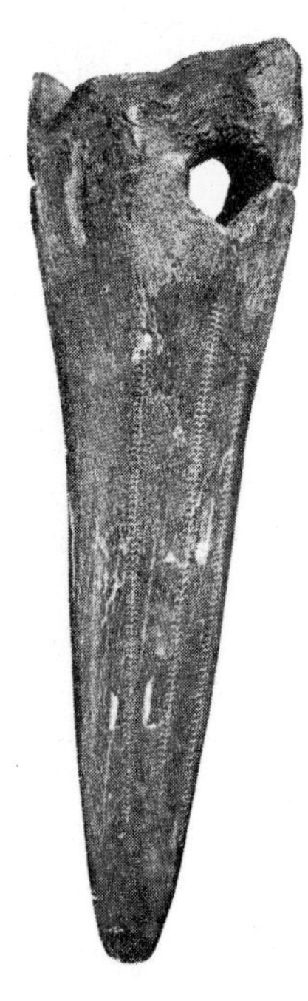

Early Stone Age bone axe-head, handsomely decorated.

Women liked to adorn themselves then, too. They made jewelry of amber. A string of beads consisting of 98 animal teeth also dating from that period was found in a grave. One is easily reminded of the large number of similar necklaces made of ceramic worn by women today. The eternal feminine relationship is clear.

Material

Cattle bone is the principal material used for making bone articles today. Horse bone is just as good and can be used in making larger objects, but it will not get as white as the former. Sheep bones are very hard and are excellent for jewelry and buttons.

If you want to do all the work yourself, rather than purchasing prepared, dry bone slabs be sure to use the marrow bone.

Saw away the joint with a hacksaw and remove the marrow.

Boil the bone in soda or lime water with approximately one teaspoon of alum added to each quart of water. Boil this for 1 to 3 hours depending on the size and fat-content of the bone. Rinse the bone well in several changes of water, and then bleach it for several days in the sun and open air. This is the old method.

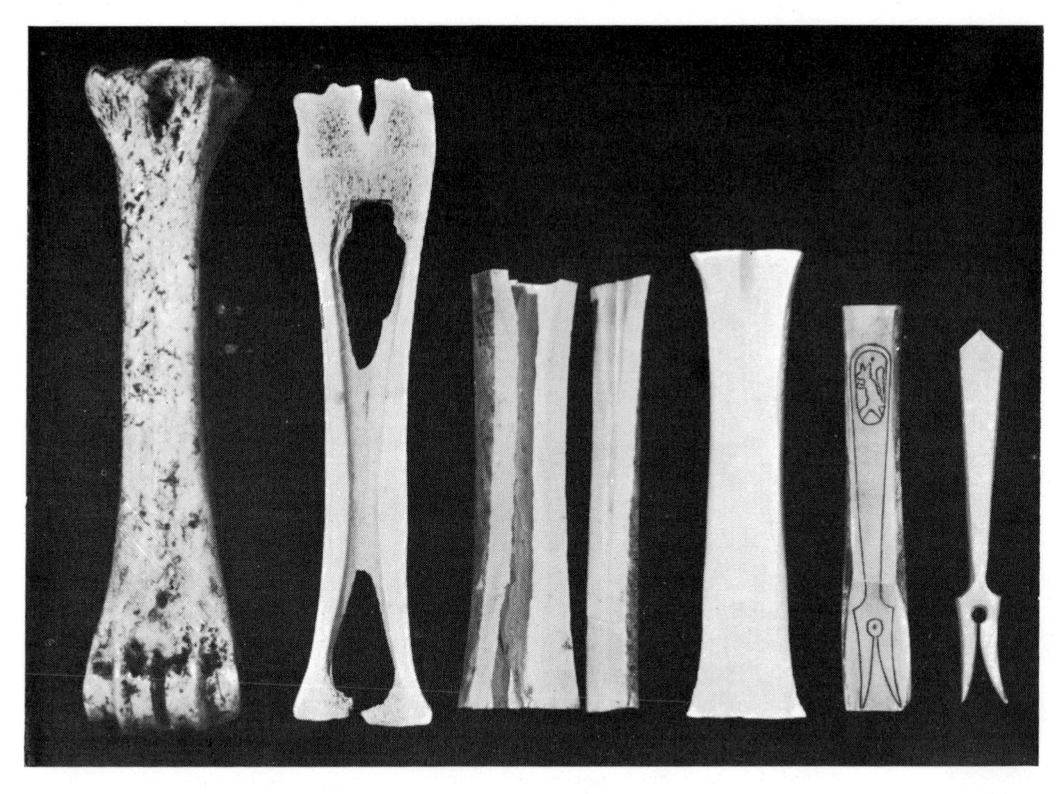

A newer method, which we think is more effective but which demands a greater degree of care, is to cut the bone into pieces of the desired size and after it has been boiled the piece is dried and ready to shape and work. Do not, however, attach other materials such as pins, wood, etc., as yet. Place it in a bleach of 40% *hydrogen peroxide* (taking care not to "burn" your fingers) for 24 to 48 hours. This method will give you the most beautiful color results.

Tools for Working in Bone

Vise

V-support for coping saw.

Saws: Hacksaw, coping saw, or jeweler's saw with blades for sawing metal.

Hand drill or brace-and-bit for metalwork.

Crosscut files, fine and coarse, with different profiles.

Jeweler's files (needle files).

File cleaner.

Gouges (for shaping spoonbowls, etc.).

Pliers, Rasp, and Hammer.

Sandpaper Nos. 1, 1/0, 2/0.

Preparation

Saw the bone lengthwise, into pieces of the desired size using a fine-toothed saw blade. Smooth the flat surface using rasp, files, and sandpaper.

If you are using old bone this work can be offensively malodorous, so you may prefer to buy treated bone slabs that have already been prepared. The bone you can buy usually comes from industrial sources and, as a rule, has been boiled out with gasoline so you can expect it to be fairly brittle. Prepared bone is sold in hobby shops and usually comes in five sizes:

No. 1—For nail files, cocktail sticks, small spoons and forks.

No. 2—Suitable for smaller handles to be mounted on stainless-steel knives, spoons, or forks.

No. 3—Best-suited for jewelry.

No. 4—For paper knives and heavier handles.

No. 5—The thickest bone is intended for heavier pieces such as salad and cake servers, etc.

Usually, the bone sections are from 4¾″ to 6½″ long. Make sure that there are no porous parts included in your finished piece. These porous parts will occur around the joints at the ends of the cut length of bone. In some bones you may find small holes going all the way through and none of this can be utilized unless you like the effect in your design.

The drawing below illustrates: 1 and 2—bones with the joints sawed off; 3 and 4—the same bones in cross-section with lines indicating where they should be cut to make slabs.

Laying Out the Design

The outline of the design and any holes, open work, or slits in the piece

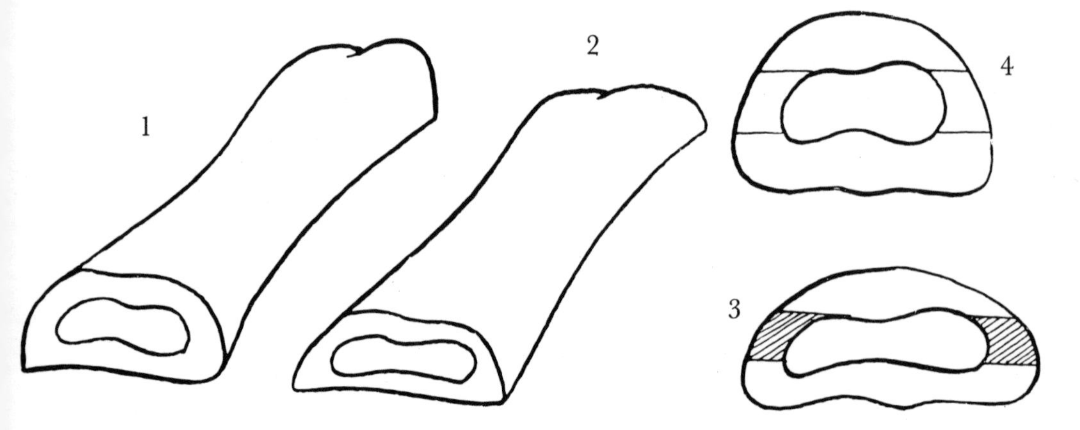

should be traced on the piece of bone. If you are using a specific drawing (such as one from this book), it will be easiest to trace the drawing on a piece of transparent paper and cement this directly to the bone. If you want to make several pieces of exactly the same design, such as a set of spoons, it is best to cut out a tracing pattern of thin wood, cardboard, or plastic. It is important to be precise in your tracing. Use a hard pencil, and keep the point sharp.

Cutting

Drill a hole for the coping saw blade. Drill this hole, if possible, at the edge of a line in a place where the hole will blend into the curve of the design. Never drill in the center of a piece that is to be sawed off. It is best to use a metalworking hand drill, and you should choose a size that suits the project at hand. While drilling use moderate pressure, otherwise you risk splitting the bottom layer of bone where the drill emerges or getting a rough area around the drill hole—both of which will make extra sanding necessary.

Sawing

You can use fairly coarse saw blades when you are working with normally simple shapes.

All delicate sawing should be done with fine metal-sawing blades.

Keep the saw moving steadily to obtain the best results, even when the lines of the design curve. The saw should be held so that it moves perpendicularly up and down its full length. The saw must work itself forward; *it must not be pushed.* Remember, this is only the front side as you saw but the finished work must look well on *both* sides.

Bone is a hard and dense material. If you push too hard on the saw blade or if you saw too fast, you can very easily overheat the blade which will make it clog or snap. The edges and surfaces of the bone piece should be carefully rounded off with a file and sandpaper. Bone meal, which always contains fat particles, will quickly clog up the teeth of the file. The finer the file, the faster it will clog. So you must keep a fine steel brush (file card or file cleaner) handy at all times for cleaning the file as you work. If it is difficult to remove the bone meal, slightly heat the file over a flame then brush the loosened particles away. Take care not to damage the file by using too much heat.

Filing and Sanding

A vise is indispensable in doing the rough filing. If you use the device mentioned here you will have an excellent tool not alone for bone work but for many other projects where the parallel jaws of the standard vise make it difficult to hold an oddly shaped piece.

A lightweight metal is best for making this small triangular block (drawing *a*). If you do not have any on hand, a hardwood such as beech would do just as well. If you make the piece of metal, drill a hole on one of the jaws of the vise, just a little bit larger in diameter than the corresponding point of the triangular piece. Drawings *b* and *c* show the hole and how this block should fit into place. If you use wood, attach a thin sheet of metal to one side of the wooden block and make use of the metal flap to support the wooden block in the vise by bending it over one jaw and down over the side of the vise. Drawing *d* shows how this is done.

In many cases the bone must be held and worked entirely in the hands. In this event it is helpful to fasten a small wooden block in the vise and

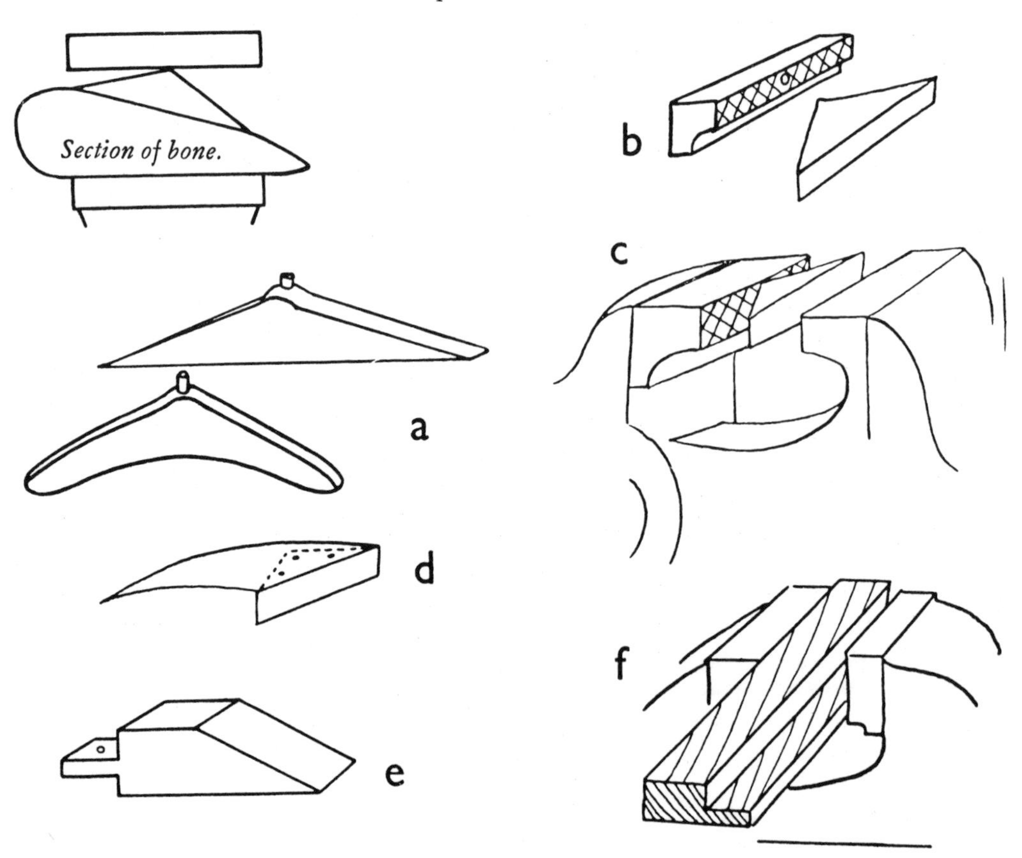

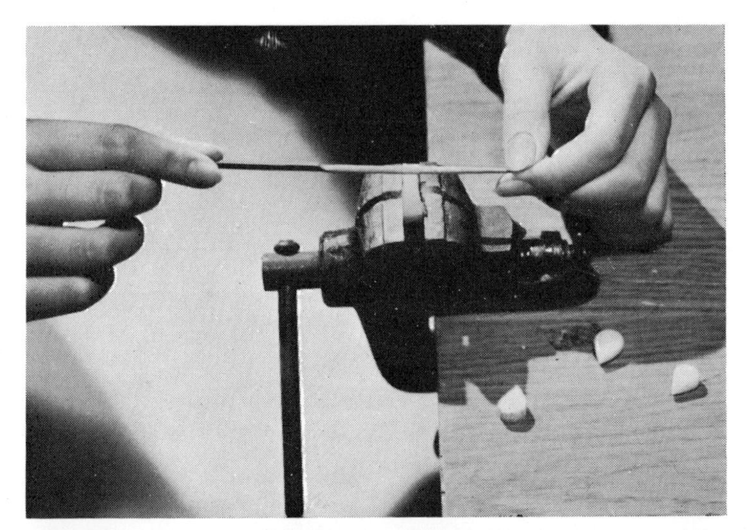

Filing.

It is difficult to fasten an irregularly shaped piece of bone in the vise, but a little triangular block, illustrated here and in the drawings opposite, will greatly facilitate the work.

Buffing and Polishing.

To avoid abrasion marks on the bone, the polishing should always be done in the lengthwise direction —never crosswise.

use that for supporting one end of the work. You can also buy a filing block, *e*, which is to be screwed to the table edge to support a piece while you are filing it. Drawing *f* shows a rabbeted wooden block fastened in the vise. This will keep the work from moving in the direction you are filing when it is propped against the rabbet.

If you turn the work slightly several times during the filing you will get an even and rounded surface.

Smooth with sandpaper, Nos. 1, 1/0, 2/0. Rub only in the lengthwise direction.

Fine steel wool Nos. 0 to 00 can be used for the last sanding before applying the polish. After this treatment there should be no visible file or sandpaper marks and you will achieve a flawless polished surface.

Bleaching

Bleach the bones after the sanding. After bleaching, the pores in the bones can be filled with an application of plaster of Paris.

Bones have varying degrees of fat content which give them their characteristic yellow color. Some people prefer the off-white color to a chalky white. If you are going to make six fruit knives, for example, most people prefer to have all the knives uniformly colored and in that case some bleaching will be necessary.

As mentioned earlier, the bleaching will be most effective if 40% hydrogen peroxide is used. The more concentrated the solution, the more effective it will be. However, you can use a less concentrated liquid and speed up the process by boiling. A 40% hydrogen peroxide solution is quite dangerous in that it will burn the skin. It is advisable, therefore, for beginners to use a 20% solution. If you do not boil it, the process takes 24 to 48 hours. After a few hours the bath becomes less potent. The solution must be stored in a dark bottle or in a dark place, and placed out of reach of children.

After the piece has been removed from the solution, rinse it well and place it out to air-dry. It can then be polished.

Polishing

Special polishing powder for bone, horn, and plastic is available in hobby shops. In addition you can use whiting or Paris white, water-ground whiting (which most hobbyists prefer for bone) or one of the various polishing and grinding powders for wood. Here you may experiment for yourself.

Hollowing Out a Spoon Bowl

After you have been working with bone for a while making paper knives, etc., it might be fun to try to make a small salt spoon.

Trace the design on a piece of bone of the desired size and fasten the bone in the vise. Using a gouge with a suitable shape form the hollow of the bowl. Bone is a harder material than wood, but the work is done in a similar manner but with more care.

Even if the hollowing work is done very smoothly, it must still be finished in exactly the same way as in other bone projects.

Bone Combined with Other Materials

Ready-made stainless steel spoons, forks, and other table service combine extremely well with bone handles. By using these stainless steel parts which are available from hobby suppliers, you need only make the proper handles for each item. Matching gravy spoons, fish forks, fruit knives, etc., can all have handles made in the same pattern. These stainless steel parts come prepared with $1/8''$ holes in the shank or with a tenon for fastening them to the formed handles.

Fastening Bowls to Bone Handles

There are two methods for fastening stainless steel knives, forks, and spoon bowls to bone handles: *embedding* and *riveting.* The method you use depends upon the size and angle of the shank extending from the implement (the shank is the part that fits into the handle), as the heavier shanks are often too thick for embedding in bone handles. If the shank is flat but too wide, it can be trimmed down by sawing a slice off *each* side with a hacksaw. Embedded shanks, however, are apt to loosen when they are soaked in hot dishwater. On the other hand, a riveted shank can be difficult for beginners to fit securely enough so that it does not wobble from side to side. A combination of these methods would therefore be the most secure, and should be used if possible.

Some of the stainless steel spoon bowls are intended only for embedding; the shanks are rounded and are not provided with rivet holes.

If your pieces do have rivet holes saw a slot in the handle with a hacksaw, making this slot the correct size and angle to fit the shank. Mark the position of the rivet holes by holding the shaft on the outside of the handle. At the bottom end the shank should be equal in width to the breadth of the handle so that it fills the sawed out slot completely.

Drilling and Embedding

A stainless steel spoon bowl, fork, or knife may come with a longer shank than is needed for embedding in the handle. The reason for this is that the same piece is prepared for use with handles of many different sizes and materials such as wood, plastic, bamboo, etc. You may need to shorten the shaft to accommodate it to your own styling.

In drilling the shaft in the handle to receive the shank, avoid drilling too far into the handle. The metal shank ideally should rest solidly against, and be supported by, an angled form at the base of the shaft rather than fitting flush against it. Use a drill-bit that has a diameter equal to the thickness of the stainless steel shank (or tenon) which is to be embedded—it is usually about 1/16″ to ⅛″—drill a row of holes as shown in the drawing as closely together as possible within the thickness of the handle. To prevent drilling too deeply make a stop on the drill with a piece of masking tape or plastic tubing placed around the drill-bit so that it can only penetrate as deeply as necessary. The thin walls which remain between the row of drilled holes can be broken through with a drill having a blunt point.

A broken or well-worn drill-bit about ⅛″ long can be used to grind away the waste walls, and form the shaft. For this job it is best to fasten the hand drill horizontally in a vise. Then bore at an angle from each side, breaking through the walls. It will be easy at the top but the bottom or inner part will be more difficult to clean out. When you can move the drill freely in the opening from side to side, you are ready to begin the embedment of the shank which should fit flush against the bottom of the slot.

If the shank is to be riveted, it can now be inserted without further ado. If the shank is intended for embedment only, before insertion roughen it with a file or scratch it with pliers to create some unevenness which will help the cement to grip the steel.

The important thing in the embedment is to use a fast-setting cement that does not easily dissolve in water or oil. One fast-setting cement is pulverized resin glue. Pour it into the hole in its liquid state; the warmed shank is next inserted as quickly as possible. You can also use the method of dipping

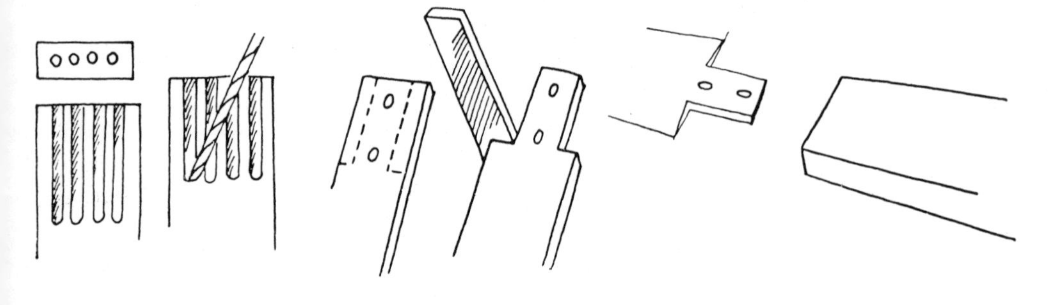

the warmed shank into resin glue and then quickly positioning it in the handle shaft.

After about an hour carefully remove the excess glue with a knife. Naturally, as the first step you must check to see that the handle and blade are not crooked but are properly positioned.

It may be difficult to obtain pulverized resin glue because it dries out and crystalizes when stored. Instead you can use litharge and glycerine. Fill the shaft with this mixture and press the metal shank down into it, cleaning off the excess which is forced out again.

Riveting

When the handle is to be attached to the shank by riveting only, it is preferable to have them both of the same width. Place the handle in a vise to stabilize it while making the slot. If it has been polished, protect the surface with a layer of thick paper or cardboard. The depth of the slot you make will depend upon the length of the shank and the position of the top rivet hole. There must be enough handle material left on both upper and lower sides of the shaft so that there is no risk of its breaking during riveting because it is too thin. The length of these slots depends on your design. The width of the slot, however, must fit the thickness of the shank very precisely. If the shank is forced into the slot it will create a tension in the bone and sooner or later the bone will break. The same breakage may occur if the slot is too open, with the shank too loose, for then the rivets will cause a tension in the opposite direction.

As a hacksaw blade is often too thin to make a slot of suitable size it is better to have a broad and flat needle file for this purpose. The two holes for the rivets should be drilled in the bone before the slot is made. It is a good idea *not* to saw the slot to its full length. Instead, make an angular shape at the base of the slot in the handle to support the shank, which has

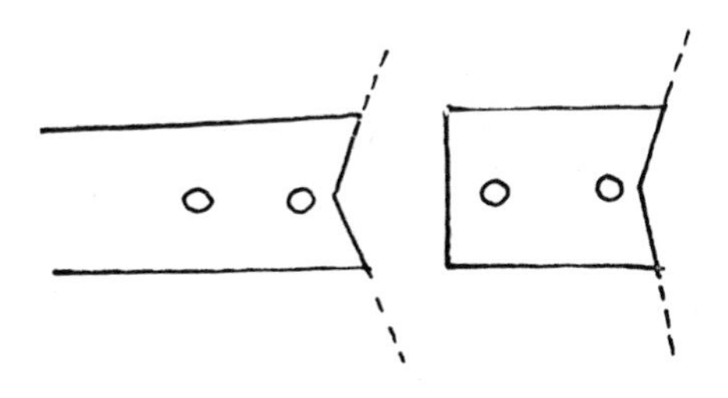

Opposite page: Drilling the handle for the shaft of the spoon and fitting the shaft. Left: Cutting the angle in the slot, described *on page 62.*

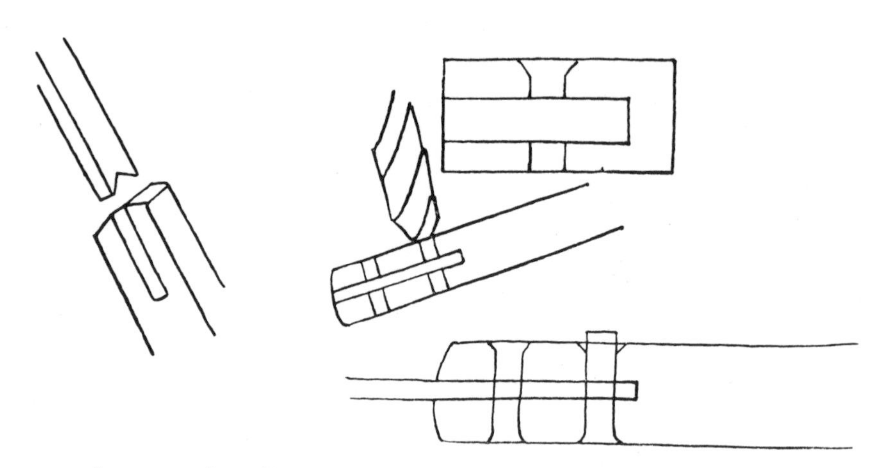

been sawed or filed, to prevent it from wobbling when the implement is used (see drawing on p. 61).

For riveting use 1/8″ aluminum wire, cut to the proper depth. It will be easier to work with if you file both ends of the rivet flat. Before inserting the rivet through handle and metal shank, you should countersink the rivet holes in the handle. Do this by a few turns of a 3/16″-5/16″ drill-bit in the hole (see drawing). This will provide space for the rivet head which is formed by carefully pounding the soft aluminum rivet when it is in place. It is always necessary to file and polish the surrounding area once more after inserting rivets.

Attaching Pin Backs

Many hobbyists have difficulty in getting a pin back to stay fast to the body of the pin. This may be because the body of the pin is too thin to support the pin back.

The pin should not be less than 3/16″ thick, and broad enough to hide the pin back. The flat bar of the pin back (see drawing) must have two holes in it so that it can be fastened to the bone with two small rivets.

The best method is to cement the fastener in place first with cellulose cement and then to carefully drill the holes. Do not use a hammer to position the rivets; use pliers in a pressing motion. Protect the front of the pin from marring, with a piece of cardboard while you are inserting rivets (see drawing, top right).

You can fasten the pin back with two small screws, but this is a more complicated job. The holes in the pin back must fit the diameter of the

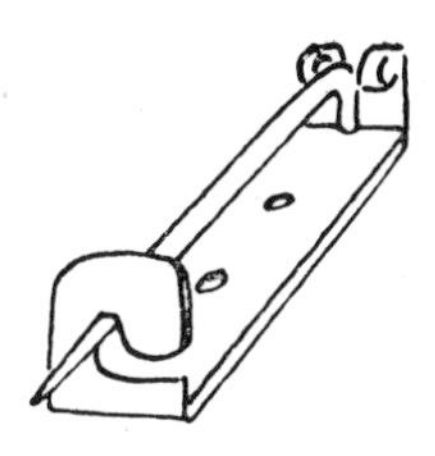

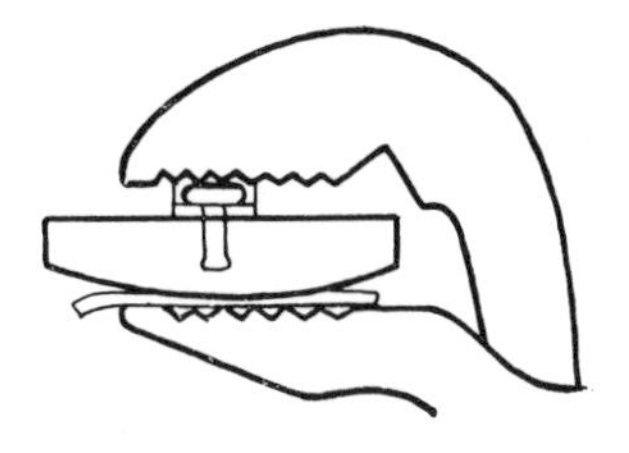

screws so that the screws can "bite." The pin back should be cemented to the bone here also, with a concentrated resin glue.

Dyeing

Bone can be dyed by boiling it in a strong aniline dye for about an hour. Experiment with the colors to find your preference.

Engraved Designs of Sealing Wax

Trace the design with a sharp, pointed knife (X-acto knife, etc.) and cut the design 1/16″ into the bone. To make round dots use metal drills of varying diameters.

The color inlay should be done with ordinary sealing wax. Some stores carry these in many colors, but others may only have black, red, and white. This will do also as the white can be melted in an old tin can and mixed to the desired hue with ordinary fabric dye powder. Melt the colored sealing wax and place it in the engraved design. A moderately warm soldering iron or a screwdriver warmed over a gas jet (remove any soot deposit with a padded glove), can be used to melt the wax and place it into the grooves of the design. It is impossible to keep the wax in the lines and holes of the pattern only but it does not matter as the entire piece will later have to be sanded with coarse, to medium, then to fine, sandpaper. Finally it is polished with a cloth. During the last polishing, should you use a rotating polishing wheel, be very careful since the heat generated can melt the sealing wax.

Working with Ivory and Whale's Teeth

Ivory is, of course, much more expensive than ordinary bone, but since you need not purchase an entire tusk the price is fairly moderate for a small piece. It is primarily used for jewelry.

Whale's teeth from the cachalot or sperm whale are short and stubby, in good supply, they are moderately priced. The narwhal's tooth or tusk, which is thin and crooked is also used, but it is not unusual to find them a few yards long, thus they are expensive. They have a more limited use than the cachalot teeth.

In olden times the long, twisted narwhal tooth was thought to belong to the fabled unicorn.

This tooth material is treated in the same way as bone, but it is not bleached. It is extremely hard to cut, but you will be richly rewarded for your efforts.

The inner core of the cachalot tooth differs in structure and color from the outer part, and this can be effectively used in the design of jewelry. You will find that in cutting ivory across the grain, the tooth structure will stand out as a beautiful network of pattern over the surface of the work.

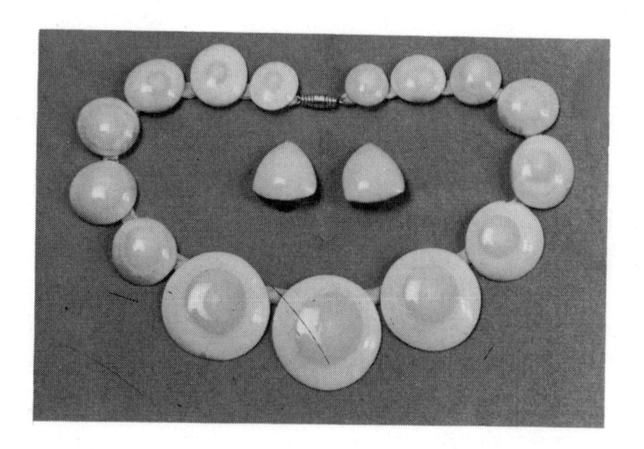

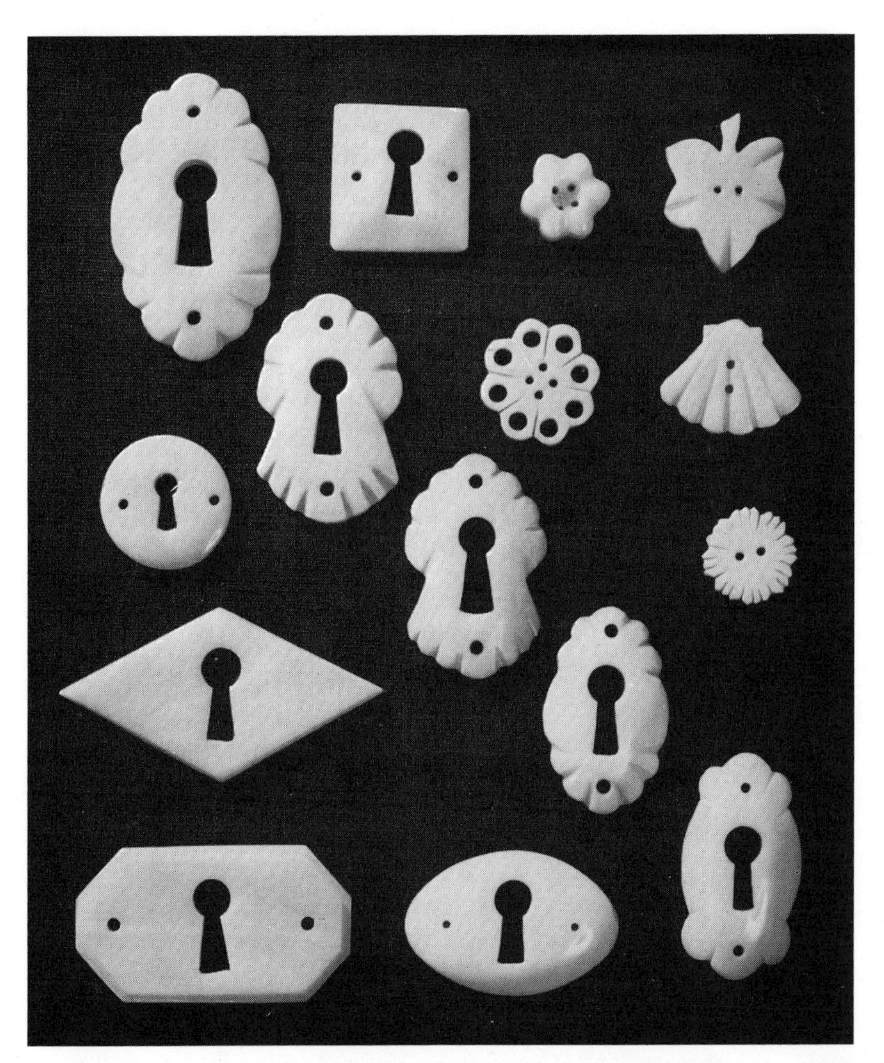

DESIGNS IN BONE

Keyhole Plates are an elegant touch to use on fine handmade wooden cabinets and boxes, the size of these keyhole plates should be determined by the size of the individual key. It is best to draw and cut out the actual keyhole shape and then design the plate around it. You will find 3/16″ a suitable thickness for the plate. The attractive bone buttons can be 1/8″ to 3/16″ thick. Decorations on both keyplates and buttons are cut with a file.

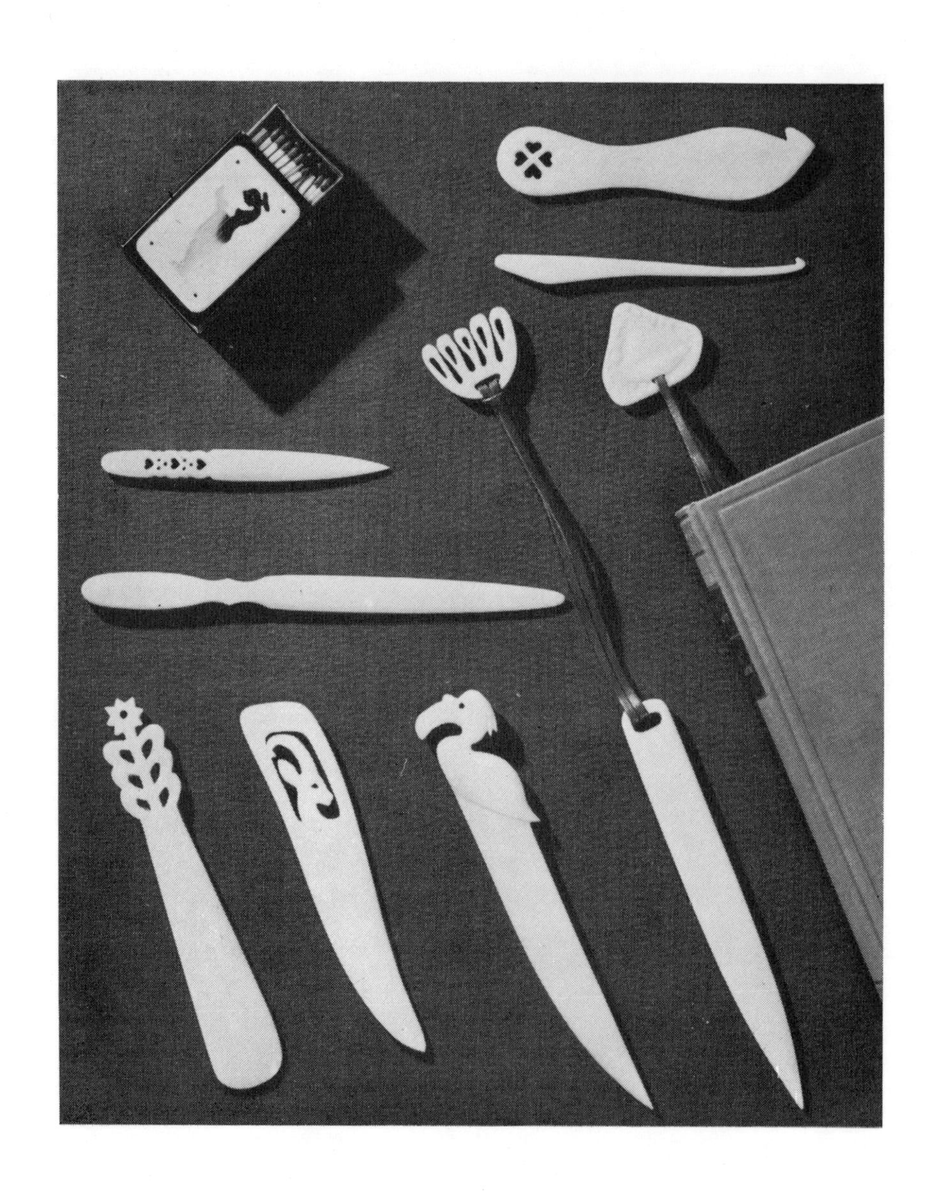

Letter Openers, Crochet Hook, Orange Peeler, Bookmarks, and Matchbox Plate

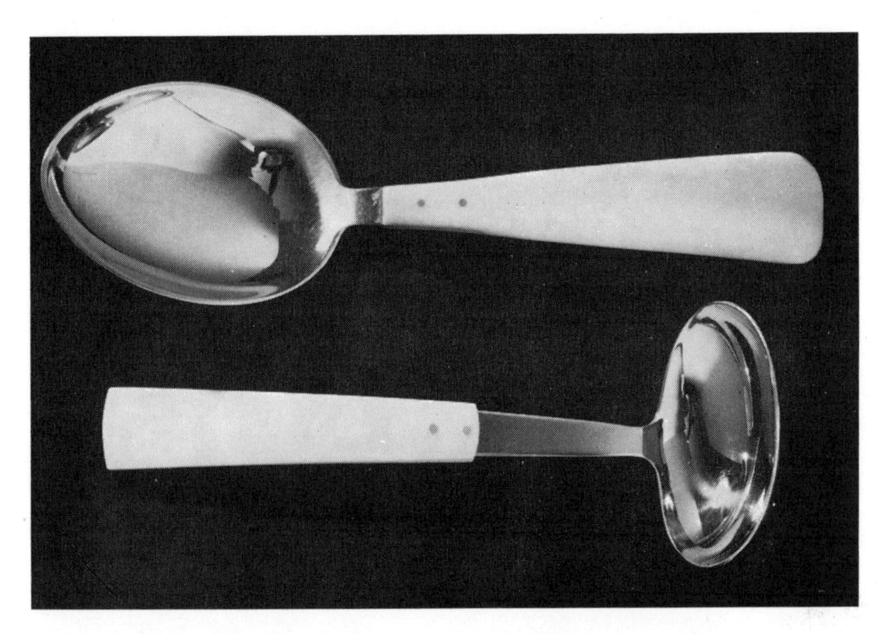

The handle is made from No. 2 size bone and is made to fit the spoon bowl and shaft. The process of forming and fastening the pieces has been described earlier. In designing the handle shape, you should consider how it fits and feels in the hand. All of the corners and edges should be rounded.

Dessert Serving Spoon and Gravy Ladle

The photograph on the opposite page shows several simple but beautiful objects which can be made of bone. The decorated bone matchbox plate is inlaid with a design of horn. The small design of horn and the bone opening to fit it can both be cut out at the same time by cementing a thin horn layer and a thin bone layer together with a piece of paper of the size of the matchbox, in between. Trace the small design and the outer shape on the bone and saw out both with a fine coping saw blade. Drill a small hole in the design to insert the saw blade. Separate the pieces and place the horn into the identical opening in the bone, then glue it into place. Polish the surface. The bone matchbox top is riveted to a thin metal sheet which is bent to fit around the standard matchbox.

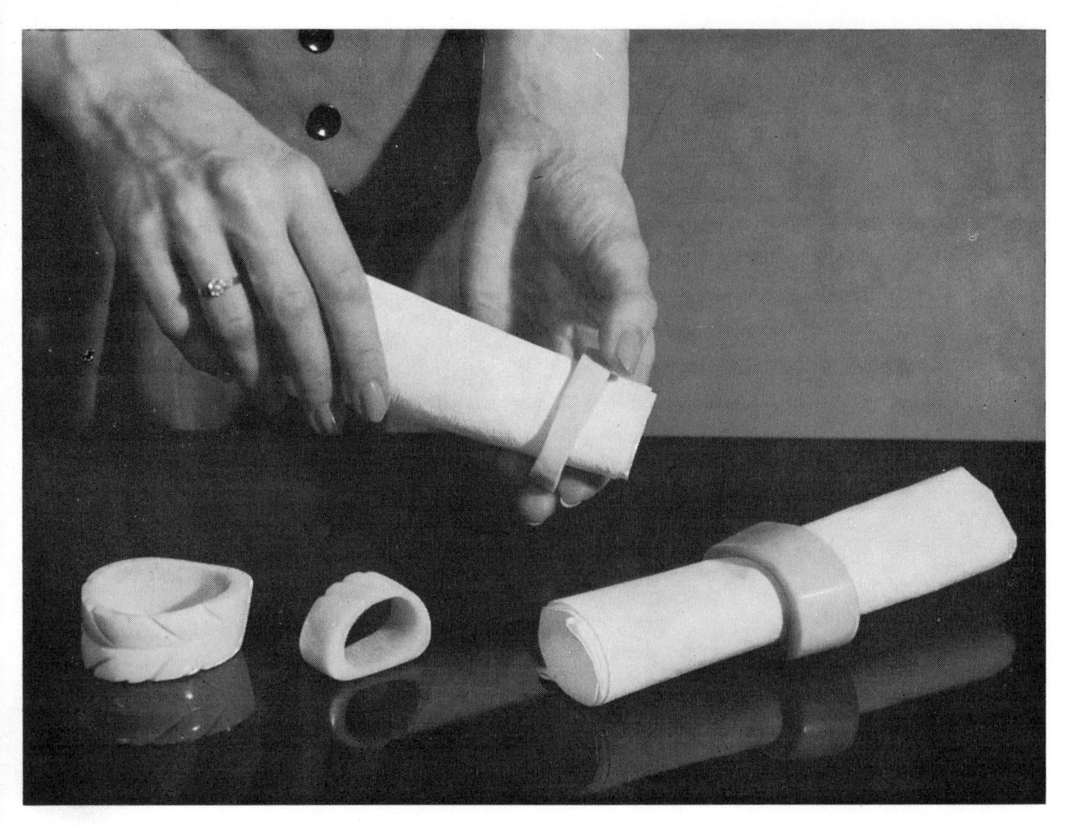

Napkin Rings

Rings of any desired width can be sawed from hollowed, smoothly bored bones. The edges are then filed and polished. Designs are made by filing them into the bone before it is polished.

Cocktail Forks and Mustard Spreader

The pieces, illustrated on page 78, will be constantly exposed to sharp condiments. Bone, quite impervious to these, is an especially good material to use. No. 1 bone is used and the piece should be about 4″ long and ⅝″ to ¾″ wide. The designs illustrated are intended as beginning samples. You should go on to discover and create new shapes and decorations, but avoid too many small details that may result in making the piece too delicate to use.

Modern Hair Clips With Engraved Design

Saw out the hair clip in the desired shape. Shown here are three different possibilities. If you have power tools, you can file the shape using a rotating sandpaper disc. Do not use a carborundum stone for this, as it will spoil it. Drill two holes with a 1/8″ drill-bit for the fastener, a piece of 1/8″ copper or brass wire which is fairly flexible. Hammer it flat at one end so that it is wider than the hole through which you insert it and is pointed at the other end to go under the hair and into the second hole. The technique for applying a wax color inlay is described on page 63. This technique is not limited to hair ornaments, but can be used on any other article of bone.

Bone jewelry looks particularly effective against solid color fabric or a nicely tanned skin. The dark portions of the two pieces of jewelry at the farthest right in the photograph are made of horn while the lighter parts are bone. The bone base of the pendant is simply made of a 3/16″ cross-section sawed from a hollowed out bone. A piece of horn is cut to fit the opening, then glued into it. Thin, dark horn plate is cut to fit the outside silhouette, pasted to the back, and offers a nice contrast to openwork designs in bone. All the other bone pieces are approximately 1/8″ to 3/16″ thick. Plastic cord of various colors is used to "string" the necklaces. Leather thongs which come in several colors are also good.

Naturalistic and abstract designs are attractive, cut in natural bone. The helmeted warrior at the left is an example of modern jewelry design following a classic prototype. To the right are naturalistic designs, decoratively handled. At the bottom are completely free, abstract forms.

Bone Jewelry Design

Working with Horn

Tyrolean horn buttons, or horn rimmed eyeglasses (these are not really horn, but tortoise shell) are the first things that come to mind when someone mentions practical objects made of horn.

But natural horn objects which were used in prehistoric times and in every age of man since that time, have served many other purposes.

Drinking vessels of horn were probably the first objects and these were still being used a generation ago, embellished with brass or silver as vessels for ink and gunpowder. The Vikings covered the stocks of their fearsome broadswords with wood or horn. The horns which summoned the village farmers to meetings were, in most cases, ordinary cow horns, similar to the ancient Shofar or booming ram's horn, used in biblical times as a battle signal or ceremonial horn and which is used to this day to announce certain religious celebrations. Horn was used from making combs to filling funnels for sausages and, as the prototype for the famous Bronze Age metal lur horns; it is one of the most versatile materials we know.

Material

The horn used for raw material here can be purchased from hobby suppliers or from a slaughterhouse. Be careful to check the horn you purchase for external flaws. Animals often damage their horns in fighting or on barbed wire fences, and these scars are sometimes deep and difficult to see. Often they will appear only after you are working on the material.

Horn objects can be made from the horn of steers, bulls, and cows. The horn of the cow differs quite markedly as it is more solid, while steer horn has only a thin shell. Horn purchased in a hobby shop is usually imported.

Working with horn is not a speedy job, and you must arm yourself with patience and begin with the very simplest designs in order to get to know the material. Then you can proceed to more complicated projects.

The horn consists of the outer shell, and the membrane which joins it to the skull. In order to use the horn as a hobby material, this inner membrane must be removed. This has already been done with the horn you will buy in hobby shops. The membrane should be removed as soon as possible, because it will soon begin to decompose, and is easily done by boiling the horn.

The horn should be completely dry before you begin to work with it or it will later warp.

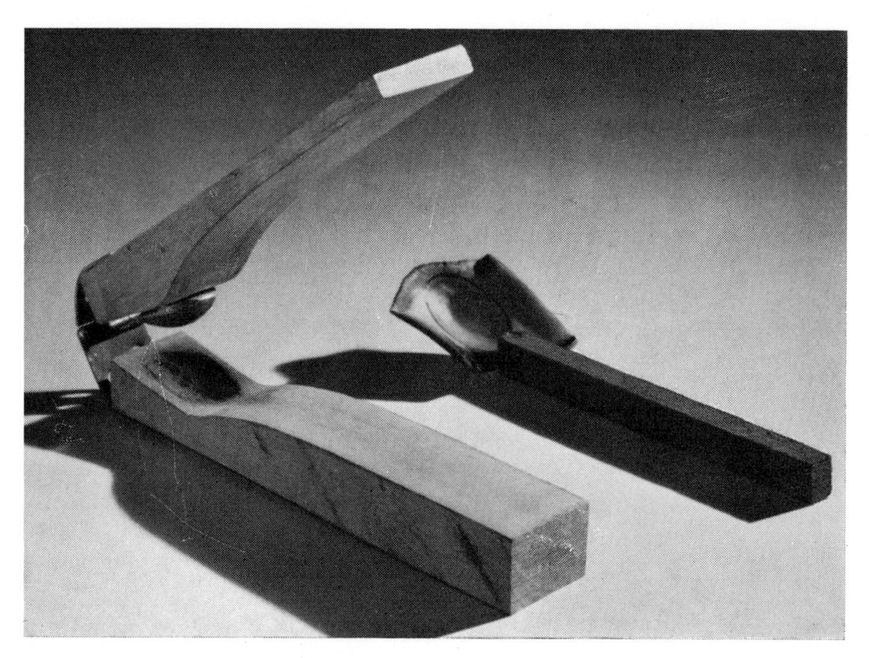

Mold or form used to shape spoon bowls such as those on page 81.

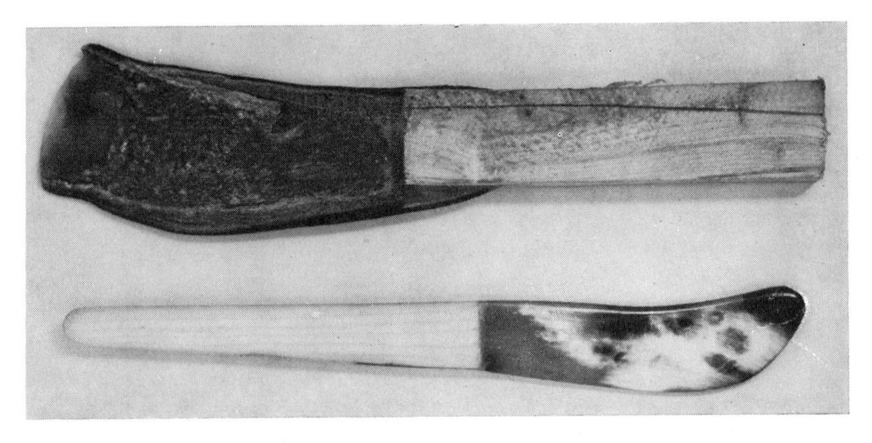

Procedure for making a butter knife: The flat piece of pressed horn is cut to fit the slot in the wooden shaft. The knife blade and shaft are then shaped.

This material is tough and strong and yet it is fairly easy to shape when it is warmed.

The different types of animal horn come in varying sizes, colors, and shapes. Therefore, the project you have in mind should determine the kind of horn that is most suitable for that use. As far as is possible you ought to take advantage of the natural shape of the horn and the play of color within it. This has been done in most of the pieces pictured here.

Tools for Working with Horn

V-support.
Saws: backsaw, coping saw or jeweler's saw with metalworking blades.
Hand drill or brace-and-bit for twist drill.
Crosscut files, fine and coarse, with different profiles.
Card file, scraper, and file-cleaning brush.
Gouge for making spoon bowls, etc., hammer, rasp, and pliers.
Sandpaper Nos. 1, 1/0, 2/0.
Steel wool.

You will also need some kind of heating apparatus for use in pressing and bending the horn—propane torch, bunsen burner, etc. A mold or form shaped for the piece that you are going to make (a spoon, for example) is needed and it may be homemade. An example of an untrimmed molded spoon bowl is shown on the preceding page.

The concave shape of the mold can be formed with a gouge. The upper, convex portion is made of tin which has been cast in a shell-shaped mold then fastened to the top piece illustrated at the top of page 73.

Preparation

The first step is to saw out the general shape and size of the pieces needed, making as much decorative use of the natural qualities of the horn as is possible.

An example of the cutting method is shown in the drawing at the top of the next page.

Before the pressing can be done, the horn must be split lengthwise (drawing 1). Remove the thick point. Straighten out the warmed horn fairly well (drawing 2). Draw the teaspoon pattern on the horn, following a paper or leather pattern. Finally, saw it out (drawing 3). If you can get a large piece of buffalo horn which is sold in most hobby shops, you can make several things from the same piece of horn.

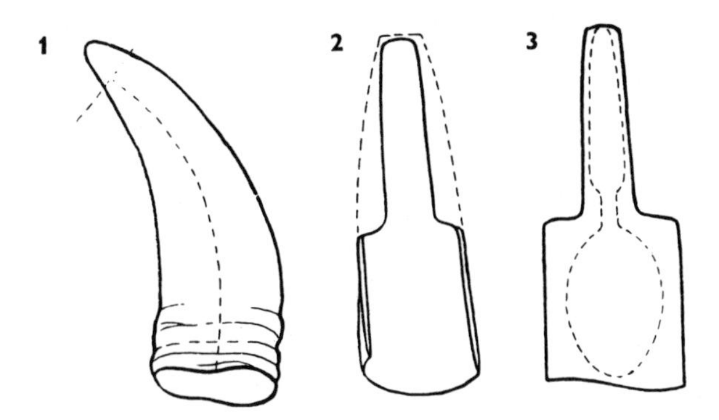

The preparation of horn is done in the same way as described in the section on plastic, but the bending and pressing techniques differ considerably.

Heating

Before heating, brush the horn with water glass (fireproofing sodium silicate dissolved in water) which will keep it from burning. When the water glass has dried, hold the horn over a flame (propane torch, bunsen jet, etc.). Move the piece back and forth so that it is evenly heated. The material may singe at the edges, but you must not allow this to happen to any area which is to be included in the finished object. If you overheat the horn it will not only change color but become brittle.

Horn softens as it is heated so that it can be formed pretty much as you like. When it cools it will retain the new shape.

Pressing

If you intend to press the horn flat to draw and work your design, heat it first then, sandwiched between two pieces of wood, fasten it securely in a vise. If it is to have some other shape, arrange it in the mold following the method shown in the photograph (p. 73) and place that in a vise or in two C-clamps to hold it in position as it cools.

As soon as the horn has thoroughly cooled, it will retain its new shape, thus, you can safely remove the press and start the finishing process.

Finishing

The first step is to saw away excess material, then refine the form with a file. If you have power tools (a turning lathe), you can attach a rotating rasp or file.

During this process you must use the tool carefully to maintain the edges of the piece, and also to even out any lumpiness on the surface of the horn, which invariably occurs.

Polishing

The special polish for plastic, bone, or horn described on page 14 should be used for finishing horn objects. You can instead simply dip it in cold water then rub it vigorously with pulverized pumice. This will effect a smooth surface. Rinse the horn free of pumice particles and rub it vigorously with a wet cloth and powdered coal (a very fine powder). This provides a warm, deep, surface shine which will be further enhanced by a final protective polishing using a paste made of soap and Paris whiting.

Horn Sculpture

The dynamic shape of a complete horn suggests a sculptural form such as the bird on page 79.

Begin by shaping the thick, pointed end of the horn to make the bird's bill. Even out any lumpy areas with a rasp so that the horn's surface is fairly uniform. You must then place the horn in a pot of water and boil it thoroughly for at least an hour. You will then find it to be soft enough to mold with the hands. Shape the figure and set it aside to dry and cool. When the material is well dried and completely cool, it will be rigid and will retain its new form.

You can do as you prefer in regard to the surface treatment, polishing the bird to a very high gloss or leaving it dull.

In either case the surface should be leveled with a flat file and rubbed with sandpaper. Cut out the waste area between the legs, wings, etc., with a sharp knife keeping in mind that extra objects can be made from good small pieces. Polish the finished piece with a chamois after giving it a final cleaning with a linen cloth and soapy water.

Working with Deer Antlers

Closely related to objects made of domestic animal horn are those made of deer antlers. The preparation technique is the same as that for bone. But here nature has uniquely determined the shape and most antlers are used in their natural form and appearance. Following are a few examples:

Saw off one branch of a small antler nearest to the thick, lower bone deposit at the base. Polish the outer surface if desired, or you may prefer to file it. This piece can be used as a handle on a carving knife, bottle opener, poultry shears, etc.

The base of the antlers can be used as a frame for a piece of jewelry by removing the thickened bone deposit and the inner membrane then smoothing the edges roughened in the sawing. Clean and polish the entire branch using one alone, or several entwined with one another for lamp bases, racks, or some similar rustic decoration.

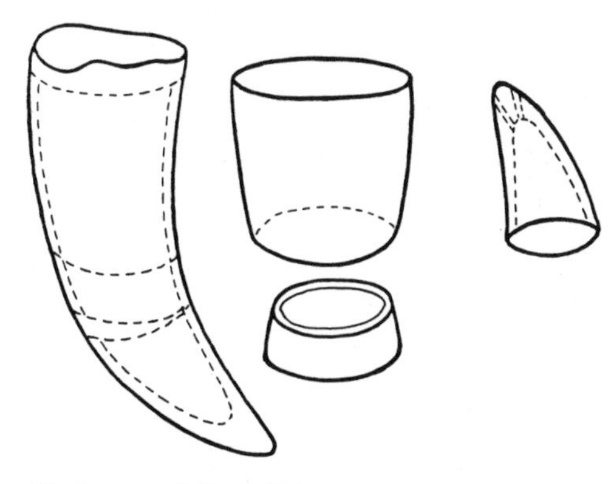

Salt and Pepper Shakers and Egg Cups

Interesting shakers are made from the tip of the antlers (see drawing above). Drill a few pouring holes in the pointed end after it has been processed. Cut a circular base plug, with a hole for filling the shaker, from 3/16″ wood and glue it into place recessed ½″ up from the bottom edge.

The pepper shaker is made to match but the pouring holes are smaller. Make the wood base plug in the same way, drilling a hole in the base and positioning it ½″ up from the bottom edge of the shaker to allow space for the cork. Tightly fit corks for both shaker plugs and be sure they do not protrude beyond the bottom recess. The shakers can be filled through the bottom hole then sealed with the corks.

The egg cups are sawed off cross-section rings. If the ring is not from the upper, *conical* part of the antler, shape it on a conical dowel rod or over a round object then, while it is still malleable, use some heavy objects to force and hold them to an oval shape until they are cooled and set.

Horn Cigarette Cups and Bone Cocktail Picks

Saw the horn cigarette cups as shown in the drawing on page 77. To stretch and thin the horn, use a piece of 1″ wood in the desired diameter of the cup and press it down into the heated horn, at the same time turning it around like a reamer while the horn is still warm. Make a wood base of 3/16″ wood and glue it into the bottom of the cup.

Cocktail picks are drawn on paper and glued to a thin bone layer. Cut out the patterns with a coping saw. Then file, sand, and polish them.

DESIGNS IN HORN

Birds

The imported, large buffalo horn has the best form and line for birds and other horn sculpture. The wading bird pictured here has its origin in African sculpture.

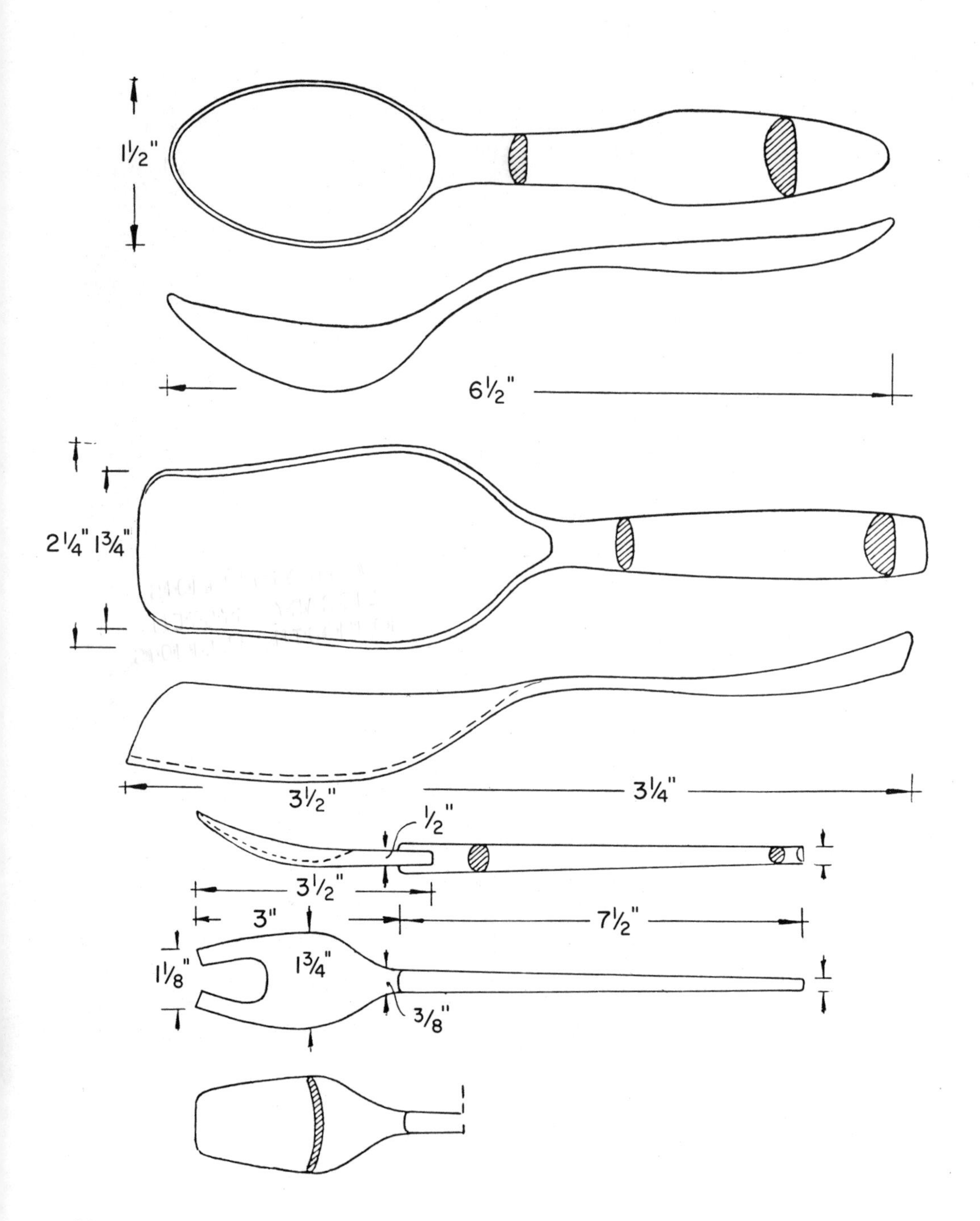

1½"
6½"
2¼" 1¾"
3½"
3¼"
½"
3½"
3"
7½"
1⅛"
1¾"
3/8"

These utensils are all constructed on the same principle. Use the following sequence as your working procedure:

a. Saw the material (see 3 drawings, p. 75).
b. Warm the horn and press it flat.
c. Draw the outline on the flattened piece and saw on this line.
d. Warm it again and place it in a prepared mold (see p. 73).
e. File and polish the surface.

Flour Scoop, Sugar Spoon, and Modern Salad Set

The pins are made from small pieces of horn (cuttings from larger projects can be used for small items and should be carefully hoarded) which have an interesting and vivid pattern. They are nicest from the side of the horn, cut to shape or pressed flat. Further shaping is done with a file; then they are sanded, polished, and fastened to a pin back (see directions, p. 62).

Some earrings are made in regular geometric shapes while others are free form, and only the basic dimensions of length and breadth need be the same. If wood or some other material is added, you should be sure that its color harmonizes with the horn. Cherry or pear wood is excellent for the purpose. If you plan to use wire, it should be of silver.

Pins and Earrings

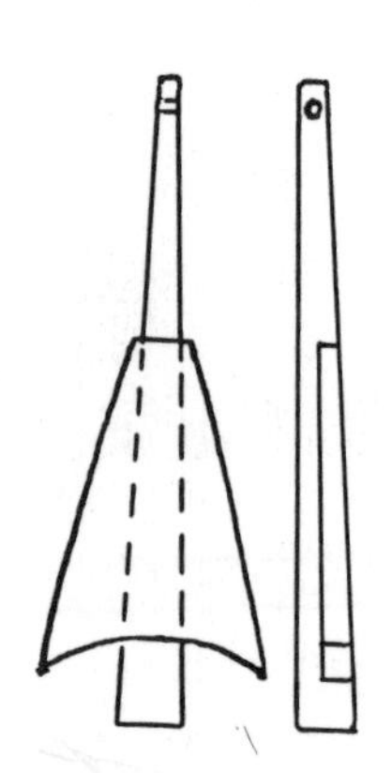

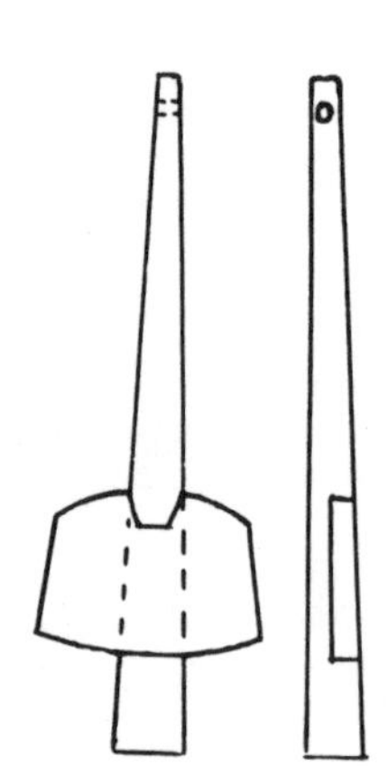

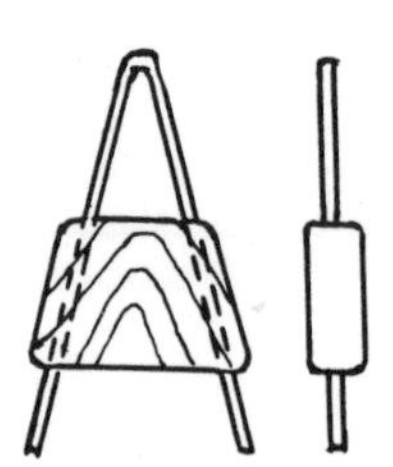

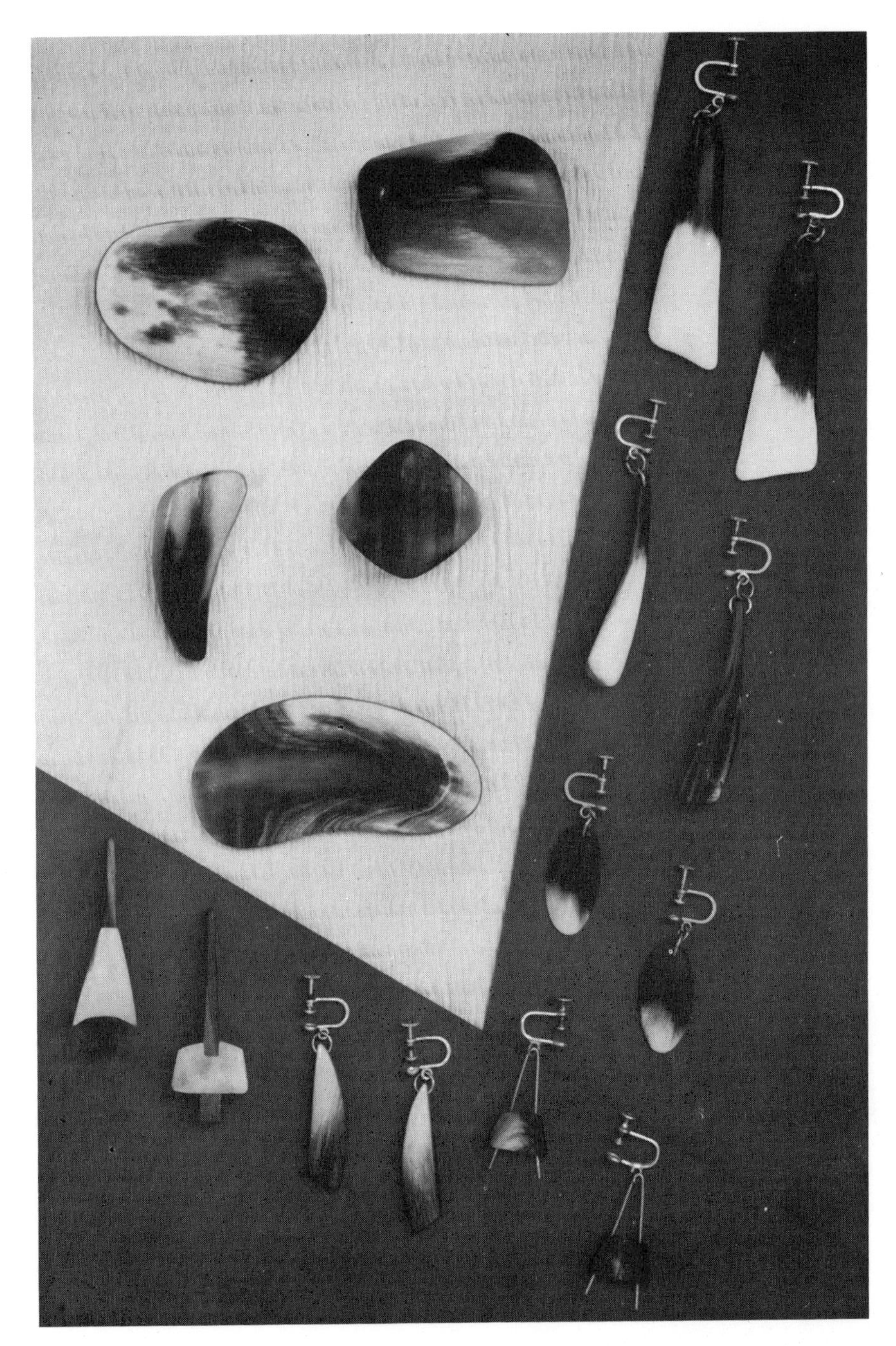

Buttons and Scarf Ring

Horn is an ideal material for buttons and is again becoming increasingly popular. The pattern and attractive color nuances of these buttons will be suitable for many types of garment. The buttons shown here are made in different ways. The light round and oval buttons at the lower left of the illustration opposite, are made of reindeer antler. Thin cross-section slices are sawed from the antler and holes are drilled through. The surface is then smoothed with sandpaper and all the edges are rounded. Reindeer antlers are not very easy to obtain, but any other antlers may be used instead. Finish the buttons by polishing them. Among the darker buttons, the one at the upper left is made of cow horn. The decorative lines in this button are cut with a saw and then filled with ordinary tin solder melted in a soldering pot. This trim is applied before the polishing is done.

The rest of the buttons are made of thin horn pieces shaped with the saw, file, and sandpaper. They are polished as all buttons must be so that they do not snag the fabric or unduly rub through the buttonhole threads.

The scarf ring (drawing, lower right) is made in the same way as the egg cup described on page 77. But be careful not to make it too large. Here you do *not* polish the inside of the piece or it will slide right off the scarf!

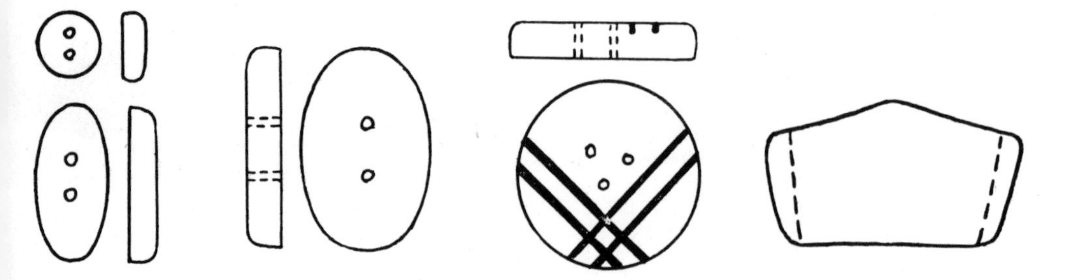

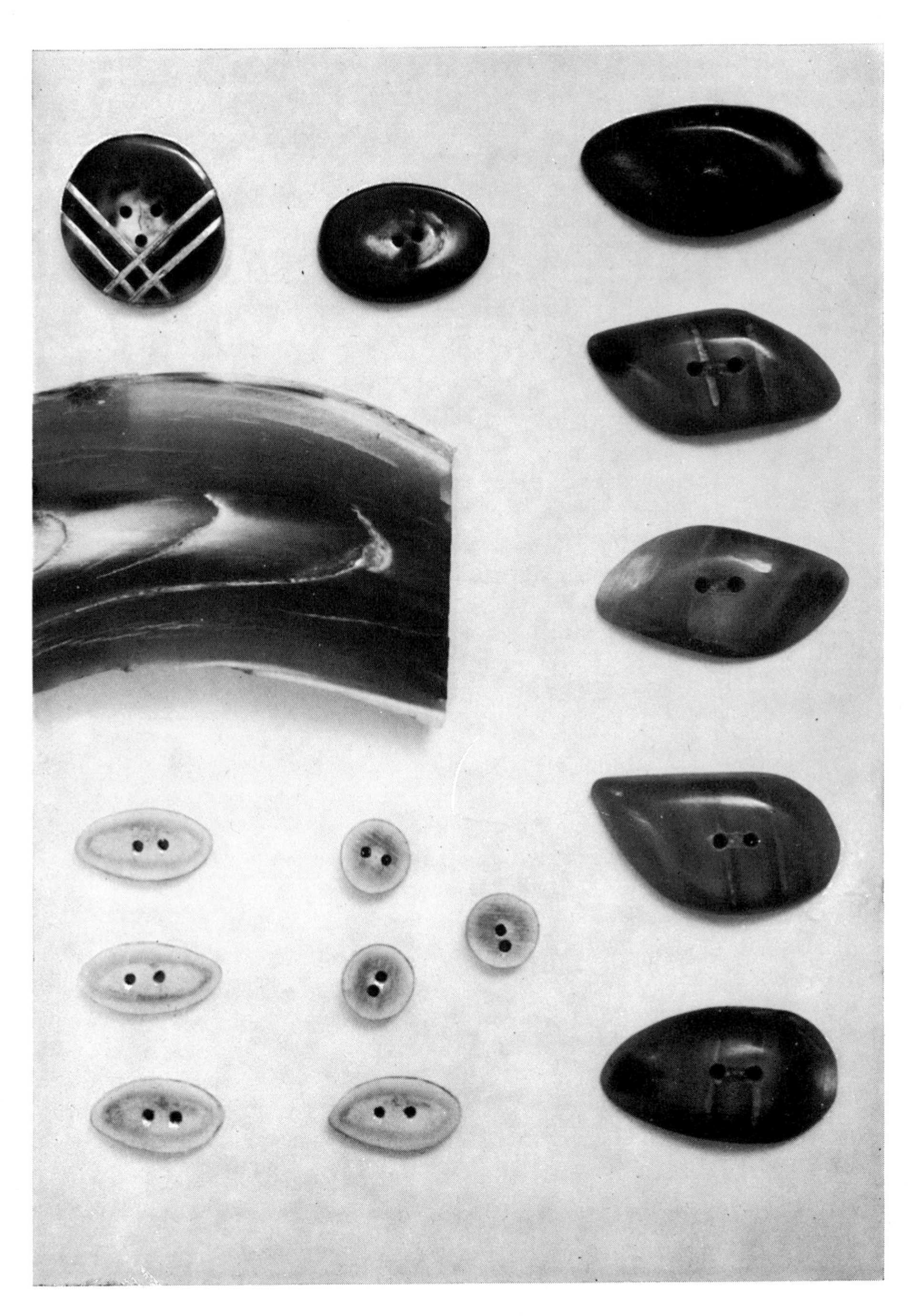

Amber - Nature's Royal "Bone"

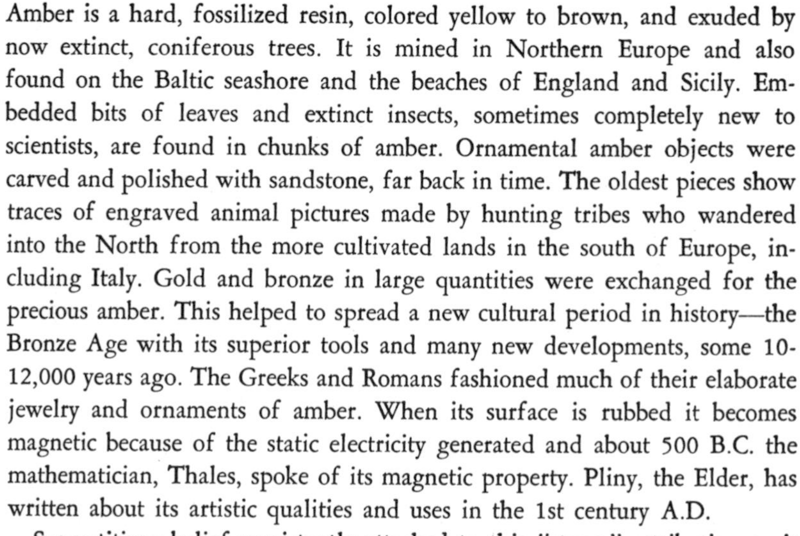

Amber is a hard, fossilized resin, colored yellow to brown, and exuded by now extinct, coniferous trees. It is mined in Northern Europe and also found on the Baltic seashore and the beaches of England and Sicily. Embedded bits of leaves and extinct insects, sometimes completely new to scientists, are found in chunks of amber. Ornamental amber objects were carved and polished with sandstone, far back in time. The oldest pieces show traces of engraved animal pictures made by hunting tribes who wandered into the North from the more cultivated lands in the south of Europe, including Italy. Gold and bronze in large quantities were exchanged for the precious amber. This helped to spread a new cultural period in history—the Bronze Age with its superior tools and many new developments, some 10-12,000 years ago. The Greeks and Romans fashioned much of their elaborate jewelry and ornaments of amber. When its surface is rubbed it becomes magnetic because of the static electricity generated and about 500 B.C. the mathematician, Thales, spoke of its magnetic property. Pliny, the Elder, has written about its artistic qualities and uses in the 1st century A.D.

This early 17th-century pitcher was carved and turned, combining several different pieces of amber. It can be seen at Rosenborg Castle, Copenhagen.

Superstitious belief persistently attached to this "stone," attributing to it powers of healing the sick, of preventing disease, and of warding off bad luck, and these have helped, perhaps, in maintaining its popularity in peasant art. During the 1800s all types of buttons, pipe stems, beads, hearts, religious articles, and other carved objects were assiduously made by peasant artisans who continue to carve in amber to the present day.

The Danish carver in amber and ivory, Lorenz Spengler, who worked during the reigns of Christian VI and his son and successor, Frederick V (who became King of Denmark and Norway in 1746), created beautiful pieces, many of which are to be seen in Copenhagen in the Rosenborg Castle collection. He mentions in some of his writings that carving in amber and ivory was a very popular pastime at the court.

Amber jewelry has recently enjoyed a renaissance and this old material is now treated with a more modern appreciation of the natural hues and decorative qualities within it. The skilled amber cutter does not force the material into shapes which are unsuited to the "stone," but he seeks in each case to find just that form of expression which best suits the piece in hand.

Material

Amber is a fossilized pine resin found washed up on the shores of Europe.

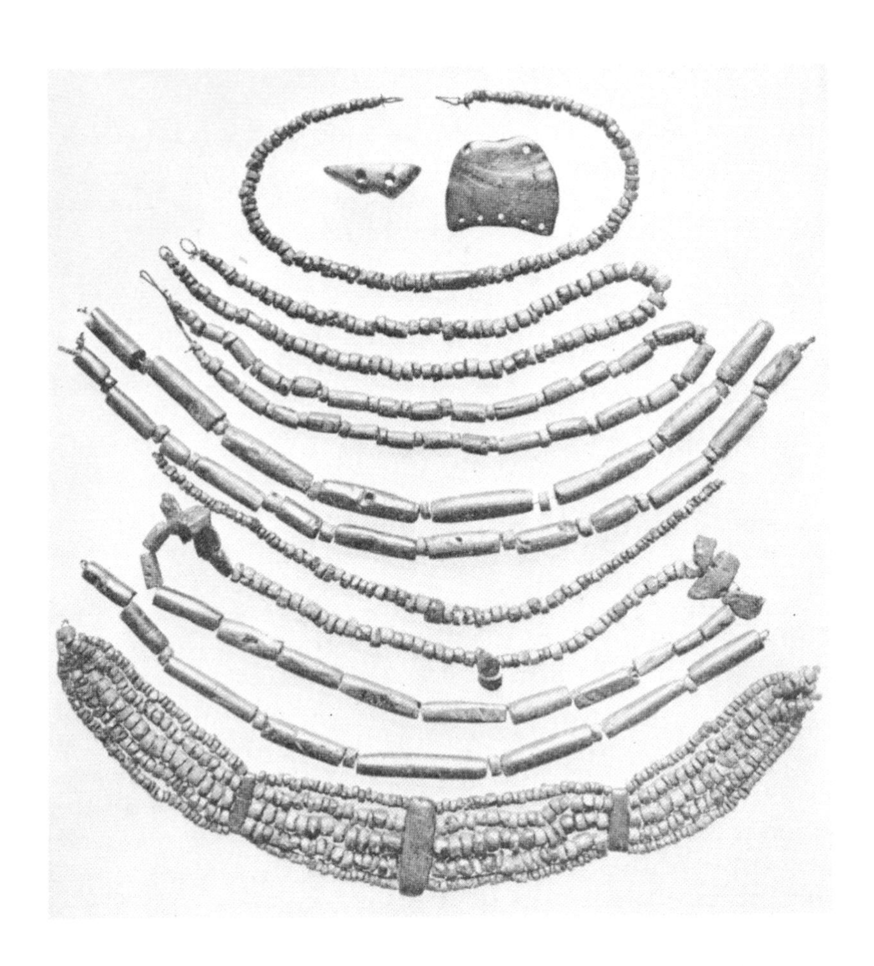

Top: Late Stone Age amber jewelry. The two small pierced objects are separator pieces for necklaces of several rows of beads such as the lower one in the photograph (National Museum, Copenhagen). At the right is an amber box c. 1700. The lid design is cut in relief (Art Handicraft Museum, Copenhagen).

An unworked piece of natural amber fitted with an eyelet and used as a pendant.

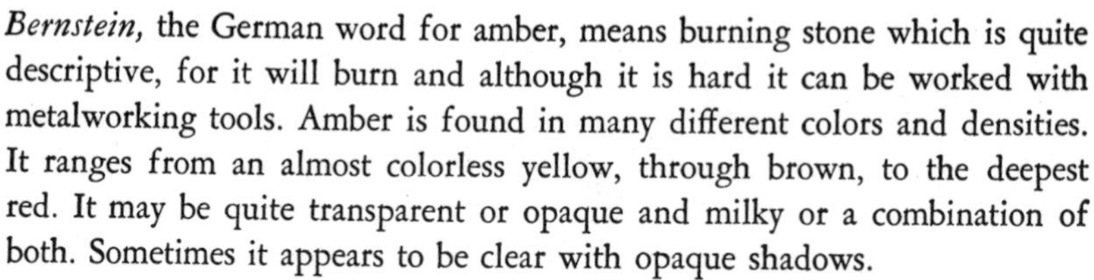

Bernstein, the German word for amber, means burning stone which is quite descriptive, for it will burn and although it is hard it can be worked with metalworking tools. Amber is found in many different colors and densities. It ranges from an almost colorless yellow, through brown, to the deepest red. It may be quite transparent or opaque and milky or a combination of both. Sometimes it appears to be clear with opaque shadows.

Flat sheets of small pressed pieces of amber are also available. They are called by different names such as antique amber, mosaic amber, or pressed amber. They are all alike in that they have a darker color than the primary form but they are useful for many different things. Be selective when buying amber or you may be paying for an unusable piece.

Tools for Amber Work:

Saws: hacksaw, coping saw or jeweler's saw, and metalworking blades.
V-support for coping saw.
Hand drill with twist drill for metal, 1/32", 1/16", 1/8".
Crosscut files, fine and coarse with different profiles.
Several needle files of different profiles.
File card or file cleaner.
Sandpaper Nos. 1¼, 1/0, 2/0.
Pliers; small, round, and flat nose.
Tweezers.

Designs

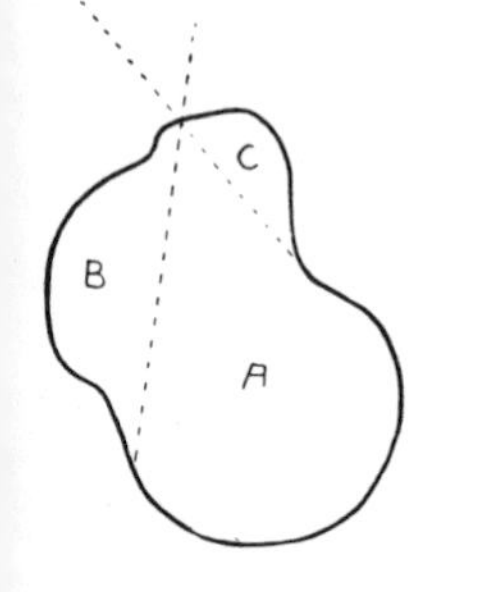

Cutting a piece of amber. A *can be used for a pendant,* B *and* C, *for earrings.*

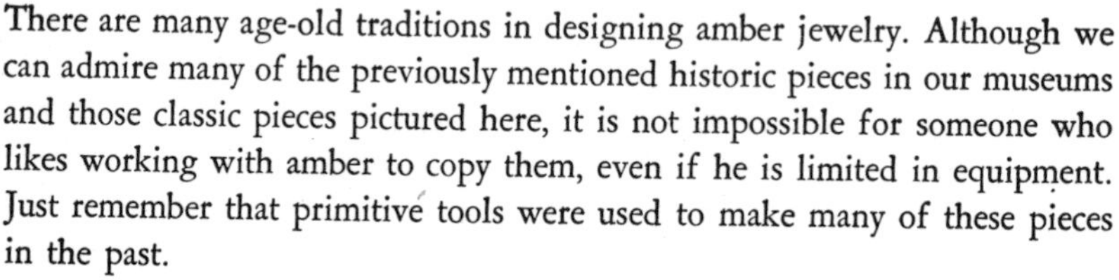

There are many age-old traditions in designing amber jewelry. Although we can admire many of the previously mentioned historic pieces in our museums and those classic pieces pictured here, it is not impossible for someone who likes working with amber to copy them, even if he is limited in equipment. Just remember that primitive tools were used to make many of these pieces in the past.

It is not at all unusual to find a piece of amber of such natural beauty that it would be a pity to "improve" it by cutting and polishing. You can simply bore a small hole, insert an eyelet and use the piece as a handsome pendant. Amber, since it is so lightweight, is very good to use for large or dangling earrings.

Preparation

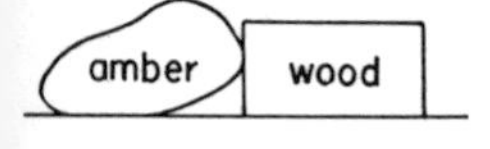

Sawing

The amber piece must not be fastened down to work it. You can nail a

wooden block to your work table and lean the amber against that (see drawing) while you cut it with a junior saw—a small version of the hacksaw—since it is probably a small piece; or use a hacksaw on a larger piece. This saw achieves the most even cut. Do not allow a saw to get stuck in the piece and possibly split it.

Forming or Shaping

Shaping is initially done with a flat file, working until the desired shape is reached, using various files as you work. Take even strokes and make each second stroke at a right angle to the first wherever possible. Finish with sandpaper (from No. 1¼ to 1/0 to 2/0) and apply this abrasion in the same way, using very light strokes at the end so it will be easier to remove every trace of the file marks.

Buffing and Polishing

Rub the piece hard with ground pumice and water. The easiest way to buff amber is to stroke it on a cloth or an old razor strop nailed to the end of the work table. Hold the other end in your left hand. Pick up the amber in your right hand and dip the piece first into the water and then into the pumice; rub it vigorously back and forth on the strop. You can always tell if the buffing powder has the right consistency as it will "bite" into the amber. But watch for any sharp edges that are meant to remain sharp. Do not let them disappear by holding the amber piece improperly.

This part of the work is very important. Your work must not be marred by deep scratches, and remember that a surface which is too rough will not polish well.

Polishing

Before starting to polish the piece, wash it thoroughly in clear running water to remove every last bit of pumice or you will hinder the shine. File marks can be removed without pumice by using a rich polishing cream instead, but this requires strength and a great deal of patience.

Dab the piece with the polishing cream, then begin to polish it with a soft cloth, at first rubbing hard and then with a lighter pressure. Devote a good long time to this job and you will be rewarded with the most beautiful and lasting results.

Drilling

The easiest way to bore through amber is to fasten the drill handle in a C-clamp or vise, with the drill-bit turned upward. Hold the amber with the left hand and turn the handle with your right hand. Do not fasten the amber piece while drilling as that will hold it too rigidly and it may split. Drill lightly and keep the drill-bit free of amber particles. Should the drill stick fast in the amber or clog, squirt a drop of oil on the bit and as a rule you will then be able to carefully feel your way out. Do not drill deeper than the length of the brad or eyelet that is to be inserted and make sure that both the brad and bit are of the same diameter.

Two bracelets, some pendants, and a pin of natural amber. Below: Several pins showing how the natural beauty of the amber has determined the design.

Planning the Jewelry Design

There are some definite rules that any jewelry designer should follow: principally, you must decide who is going to wear the article you are making. A thin, tightfitting necklace on a large neck, or a narrow ring on a heavy hand give the impression that the jewelry is cutting into the flesh. A broad face should not be made still wider with large earrings, and a long face should not be further elongated with a pair of long, dangling earrings. A tiny pearl on a very large ear looks lost. Unfortunately, these simple rules are too often disregarded, although on some people any effect can be striking, even though you would normally consider a particular design too bold. You will be wise to create a suitable design at first, for the person you have in mind. Create something new rather than follow the fad of the day. The odd shapes of amber chunks readily suggest new designs.

Pendants should be ground to a teardrop shape, or the natural shape of the piece simply modified so that the weight rests at the bottom of the pendant, and the distinctive natural beauty of the stone is, for the most part, retained as the principal decorative element.

Amber hearts are probably one of the most popular designs for this jewelry material. Originally this was a "sweetheart" gift which was carved and polished during long winter evenings.

If you want to make an attractive heart of amber, it must not be too thin. Seen from above its circumference resembles an elipse. If you are not able to make the right and left halves exactly the same by visual measure, grind them flat on both sides keeping the thickness. Draw the shape exactly to size on a piece of paper, cut this out and draw or cement it right on the amber. Now make the heart shape by filing and sawing the shape. The notch at the top is most easily made with a 3-sided file. Now the heart can be evenly rounded off. Grinding an amber heart is not easy and it should not be the first project attempted in amber.

Necklaces can be made in many different ways and styles; using beads of graduated size, in strands of different lengths, and also grouped together with strand separators placed at intervals (see illustration, p. 87). Popular too, are necklaces made of raw amber chunks which are just cleaned to remove accumulated oil and dirt. To avoid splitting the bead, drill from one side to the middle, and then from the other side, carefully, so the channel meets exactly in a straight line.

Beads can be assembled using those of one color, either clear or milky, but mixing the variegated types can also be very effective. They should be threaded on silk thread made especially for the purpose, not nylon which is difficult to work with. A professional look is obtained by using a pair of silver end beads which have an eyelet for the fasteners (see drawn enlargement). To fasten the thread in the bead, cut it to 1/4" beyond the last bead and dip it in some shellac which will stiffen it. (Stiffening the end is a help in threading any beads for a necklace.) Hold the silver bead in a needle-nose plier over a source of low heat until it is quite hot then quickly insert the end of the thread. The shellac will melt and if the thread is forced further in it will form a tiny ball which will set in the shellac as it cools.

Earrings

It is fun to make earrings of amber and as far as is possible they should be cut from the same piece so they are similar in pattern. Shape them in a mirror image of each other and bore the eyelet with great care as it is so small, usually 1/8" or less, in diameter (see findings, p. 94).

Ear clips can be uniformly rounded quite easily but it is a little more difficult to match curved surfaces on both. Cut out two equal pieces of amber, file the outline shape and round them out with a file working from the outer part to the center. The back must be flat unless it is to dangle, and need not be pasted or screwed to the earring back. When positioning the amber to fit the back, it must hide the shank so it does not show when worn on the ear.

Pins are ground much like the earrings. Drill holes on the wrong side for the pin backs which come in various styles. Place the pin back a bit above the predominant axis of the piece so that the pin will not tip forward when it is worn. Also remember that the point of the pin should be to your left so you can insert it with your right hand as a guide.

Rings are usually ground to a cabochon shape and held in dull settings. This is not necessary for you can make your own design for the setting to compliment your amber, take it and your "stone" to a good jeweler who will execute it for you at a moderate price.

Bracelets can also be made of natural pieces of amber by either drilling a hole (as in the beads) or cutting flat pieces in matching thickness. In the latter case the pieces must be cut, ground, and polished before they are drilled to avoid breakage. Make two parallel channels (diameter about 3/32″-1/8″) and file a bevel at each side so that the beads will fit closely together, strung on elastic thread. Make an extra large entrance to the two channels at one side of *one* bead where the knots in the elastic can be hidden (see drawing).

Buttons were sweetheart gifts in former days, particularly among the peasants of Scandinavia. Good collections of peasant culture and folk art will usually include buttons in many designs and shapes from round to triangular. Although these designs seem rather old-fashioned to us today, amber buttons add a luxurious look to handwoven or knitted garments.

Machine Grinding and Polishing

If you have an electric motor, you can equip it with a round wooden disc to which you have glued a layer of coarse sandpaper and use this for your grinding. For polishing, use a cloth buff as described in the section on plastic.

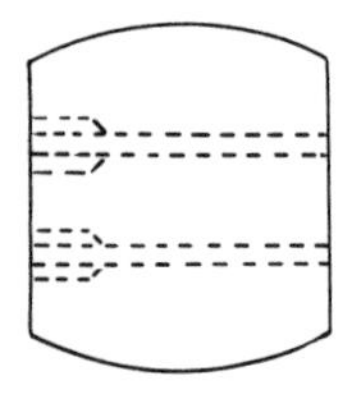

Findings

Metal findings such as earring clips, cufflinks and pin backs, as well as cup settings to hold stones for bracelets, pendants, etc., for the various small pieces of jewelry you make of amber, can be purchased in hobby shops. It is important to check them to see that they are all equipped with rivet holes or screw threading. There is no assurance as to how long an earring will remain glued to the backing no matter how good the glue.

Drill holes are filled with glue or warm shellac. Spin out the shellac to a thin thread and insert this in the hole. Take the metal rivet for the earring back (or other finding), warm it slightly then insert it into the shellac-filled hole. The shellac around the hot metal will then melt and hold it, fastened securely, in place.

In addition to the examples of amber work described here, there are countless other useful and artistic things such as bookmarks, carved desk and room ornaments, etc. that can be similarly made. The photographs should trigger your imagination and help inspire you to create your own individual designs.

A little insect that was caught and embedded in the amber when it was a fresh resin millions of years ago is a rare find, but the amber will often prove to have a defect in the area around the insect and will break easily at that point.

This little insect, indistinguishable from those we see today, was caught in a drop of resin millions of years ago.

List of Suppliers

Allcraft Tool & Supply Company, Inc., 15 West 45th Street, New York, N. Y. 10036.
All craft hand and power tools, gemstones, horn, jewelry findings.

American Handicrafts Co., Inc., 384 Fifth Avenue, New York, N. Y.
Complete line of Arts & Crafts supplies.

Astro Minerals Ltd., 155 East 34th Street, New York, N. Y.
Amber, gemstones, ivory, whale's teeth.

Butterfly Art Jewelry Inc., 291 East 98th Street, Brooklyn, New York.
Dried butterflies, insects, hobby supply kits.

Cadillac Plastics Co., Inc., 14-51 Broadway, Long Island City, N. Y. 6.
Plexiglas sheet, rods, and tubes.

International Gem Corporation, 15 Maiden Lane, New York, N. Y.
Amber, bone, gems, horn, ivory, lapidary equipment.

Carved designs in bone.